THE VOLCANO AND AFTER

PITT POETRY SERIES

Ed Ochester, Editor

THE VOLCANO AND AFTER

Selected and New Poems, 2002–2019

ALICIA SUSKIN OSTRIKER

University of Pittsburgh Press

Published by the University of Pittsburgh Press, Pittsburgh, Pa., 15260
Copyright © 2020, Alicia Suskin Ostriker
All rights reserved
Manufactured in the United States of America
Printed on acid-free paper
10 9 8 7 6 5 4 3 2 1

ISBN 13: 978-0-8229-4640-3
ISBN 10: 0-8229-4640-8

Cover art: Diane Burko, *Pu'u O'u Nightsparks*, 2000. Oil on canvas, 74" x 48". © Diane Burko.
Cover design: Melissa Dias-Mandoly

CONTENTS

No Heaven (2005)

The Book of Seventy (2009)

At the Revelation Restaurant (2010)

The Old Woman, the Tulip, and the Dog (2014)

Waiting for the Light (2017)

Approaching Eighty: New Poems

THE UNMASKING

I have come to sow the seed of light in the world
To unmask the God who disguises Himself as world

—ABRAHAM JOSHUA HESCHEL

kh'bin gekumin zayen zeyen in der velt, says the holy man
I have come for this, I have come for that, says the Baal Shem Tov
but as for me I have come to tread in the brown tar of your cities
        and I have come to watch light glitter on automobile graveyards
I have come to kiss under a beech with bark of elephant skin
        and I have come to sob under elm wineglasses
I have come to worship reflections of traveling cumulus in architectural glass
        and I have come to adore the khaki blankets of homeless men
I have come to sniff dried blood in the newsprint
        and I have come to swim like a virus down electromagnetic tunnels
I have come to pray like Hannah moving my lips sitting on asphalt
        and I have come to rave like Jonah in beery ballparks
I have come with my child to your hysterical stock exchanges
        and I have come with my grandchild to your hypocritical congresses
I have come to exchange curse for curse with the sanctimonious microphone
        and I have come to return your bronze medals
I have come in humility to beg and scratch in the dust
of your mass graves until you rise up
and I have come to defecate
in your chapels

until the death of the word "until"
I don't want you to be proven scientifically, I want you to appear
to me and to all peoples in your true form
of ruthless radiance

PREFACE

Tell me a story.

In this century, and moment, of mania,
Tell me a story.

Make it a story of great distances, and starlight.

The name of the story will be Time,
But you must not pronounce its name.

Tell me a story of deep delight.

—ROBERT PENN WARREN

Some stories have endings, and some do not have endings, at least not yet. The story of this volume has no ending yet.

It draws from six earlier books, published from my mid-sixties to the start of my eighties. There is a kind of pattern in all these books, and in this entire collection, that tends to slide restlessly, again and again, between poems invoking some sort of ideal, some sort of spiritual quest, some sort of abstraction or theory, and poems churning through the physical world. The world of things. Thickness of things. Ideal and real, spiritual and physical, clean hands and dirty hands. Hands in the dirt. The spiritual world inhabiting the physical world. Inhabit, from Latin habitare, to dwell. As Adrienne Rich says, "not somewhere else, but here." Also a tide coming in serenely bearing some of the gifts of age, some of the sorrows.

*

The volcano sequence reflects an ongoing spiritual quest struggling with a "you" who is sometimes the God of the Bible, sometimes my mother. When these poems first began to materialize, they disturbed me; I wanted to hide from them, and from myself. So I made a deal with the poems: if you agree to keep arriving, I agree not to tell you what to say. That process lasted a year, in which the poems were essentially channeled, and then another year of tidying.

Channel, from Latin canelis, pipe or groove, canna, reed. The book begins in anger against both God and my mother. It travels toward love by invoking the

Shekhina, whose name is from a Hebrew word meaning "dwelling." We might say inhabiting. In Kabbala, the tradition of Jewish mysticism, the Shekhina is God's Presence among us, or the female aspect of God. She may also be identified with my mother and all mothers. But in the material world she is exiled, amnesiac, mute—the repressed sacred female who one day may be reborn.

With two exceptions, I have not included poems from volcano that were earlier reprinted in The Book of Life: Selected Jewish Poems, 1979–2011. The poems selected for that volume primarily wrestle with God. The poems in the present volume are primarily encounters with the Mother.

All my writing since volcano, whether prose or poetry, relates to it in some way. No Heaven is a kind of rebound book. "Without contraries is no progression," Blake says, and I needed to put the spiritual quest on hold. Enough. Dayenu. I was exhausted by it. No Heaven takes a deep secular breath and engages the abundant bonds of earthly life—the life of the sensual body, the family, America's broken body politic, the history of the Holocaust and of a divided Israel/Palestine, homage to some artists and musicians I revere, and the necessity of going on "even the day our masters start a war."

The Shekhina is not named in this book, yet she inhabits it. She may be its muse. During the writing of this book my mother died, 9/11 happened, and the United States plunged into the madness of needless, unprovoked war. In a way, although my life was entirely comfortable, I was at my wits' end. We were "waist deep in the big muddy, but the big fool said to push on," as we used to sing about Vietnam, although the landscape of Iraq was not mud but the desert. The poem "Elegy before a War" experiences the personal and the political traumas as completely and tragically entangled.

In The Book of Seventy, whose title is self-explanatory, certain stylistic changes take place. An extended gaze into the mirror of mortality yields a craving for clarity, austerity, transparency. A degree of calm may be attained after decades of turbulence. This is in fact what happened to me. In the years after retirement, I began teaching part-time, the familiar tensions of anxiety that frightened me physically and emotionally grew quieter, and I found myself enjoying stretches of surprising tranquility. The aesthetic models now run from the ecstatic late work of de Kooning and Matisse, to the Atlantic tides. We elect Barak Obama as president of the United States. But the Iraq War is still on and it is still devastating. The war in Afghanistan continues with no end in sight.

At the Revelation Restaurant is partly a set of lyrical digressions on love, partly a set of riffs on the art of poetry, composed with my students in mind.

The Old Woman, the Tulip, and the Dog is a book of three voices, three personalities, that arrived unbidden one midwinter night when insomnia drove me to my study. The computer in my study is my best friend, my therapist, almost a portion of my body. It knows me better than I know myself. On this occasion it wrote the opening stanza of "The Blessing of the Old Woman, the Tulip, and the

Dog," then it paused and wrote the second stanza, paused again and wrote the third. I was entertained by the comedy of this poem, thinking it was like nothing I had ever written before, or would ever write again. Nonetheless, people liked "Blessing," and I liked them liking it. Then a couple of years later these three characters began returning with things to say, until I understood they wanted to be a book. What do they represent? I cannot tell, I merely listened. Are they id, ego, and super-ego? I don't know. I feel they are simply themselves. This is a perfect example of the poet not planning, not knowing what she is doing, but letting it occur, like lying where beach meets ocean and letting the ripples rinse you. Dualisms wash away, and you float on a tide that feels strangely like wisdom.

Waiting for the Light commenced when my husband and I returned to our roots as native New Yorkers after living for fifty years in Princeton, New Jersey. Its locale is at first the upper west side of Manhattan and then the world. The corrupt city, the corrupt world, in which nonetheless certain migrant energies continue to manifest, certain unanswerable questions continue to be posed. As a daughter of Walt Whitman, attached to the exuberance of Williams and Ginsberg, I attempt to hook the holy spectacle of things, no ideas but in things, in the America I somehow continue to cherish.

Approaching Eighty is my generic title for the new work in this volume, poems not previously published in book form. These poems contemplate change, personal and public. They sell a house lived in for forty years. They puzzle over the nature of poetry. They respond to particular moments in our collective history, including moments when you want to scream your anger and despair and not stop screaming. One of these poems looks back at my response to the First Gulf War. Some respond to the election of Donald Trump as president of the United States. The suite "Eleanor" is a tribute to Eleanor Roosevelt that sets the bar of moral heroism high. Metaphors for aging and death recur throughout, as if through a window I have left open. My mother still haunts my poems, now as she did thirty years ago. Can I now welcome her? Where is the deep delight? The deep delight is in writing the unwritten.

THE VOLCANO AND AFTER

the volcano sequence (2002)

*

Only in the space of this dialogue does that which is addressed
take form and gather around the I who is addressing it.

—PAUL CELAN

PRELUDE: VOLCANO

Let me speak it to you in a whisper
I am like a volcano
that has blown itself
out of the water

my long stony curve
my melancholiac cliffs
a strip of old hard
exoskeleton

the blue Aegean flows
in and out of me
the tourists come, oh they come
to stand where the lava flew

to imagine how
the earth roared showed teeth
bucked and heaved
to look for an hour

at where the tidal wave began
that destroyed Atlantis
and created a myth

      ***

A woman looked at my poem. What is a volcano? She wanted to know. What
    makes you like a volcano? What would the world be like without the myth
    of Atlantis?

the volcano is a crack in the earth
the volcano is a bulge over a crack
a fault line runs under it

something terrible happens
and the magma
coughs out

hot beauty
thick and magnificent rage
so what if afterward

everything is dead

***

When I was a child
I was an island
a small round bushy island
inside me were many

roots, rocks, ores,
flowings and crevasses wrinkled
pushing like joy, like fear's thin
fluids, like love's neediness

maybe too much
and somehow they all turned
to anger and for years
the lava poured and poured

righteously
destroying all
in its path
righteously

roaring

FUGUE: MOTHER

Honor your mother
what if it commanded only that
honor your mother

against nature which
bids you flee her
honor while despising

while wrestling free
while avenging
this unasked for

gift of life

    ***

Unasked for disappointing hateful life
it is the mother's fault

we fall from her space into the world
webs of organs helpless

what a pity she does not eat us
and be done with it

rats do
lions do

in dry times

    ***

Although I have put an ocean between us
still do you know how I lie awake at night
the eye in my right palm pictures you
sitting amid your litter, feet buried
by accumulated jars of buttons,
glasses lost beneath a decade of bank statements
and funny poems, penciled in margins

like the tiniest of insects,
hands folded under your chin, staring
at nothing, preparing to be blind
and helpless, for fifty years
it has tortured me that I cannot save you from madness
and that I do not love you enough

what is enough
nothing is enough

***

Someone named *he* has organized it all
the absent mathematician
the endless one
or so they say
those who believe in logic and reason
a world of equations where nothing is wasted

it may be as they suppose

what I find in the foreground is *you*
monologist, mistress of futility
loudly denouncing your many enemies
boiling through cycles of fat and thin
nervously sorting changeless debris
rags, furniture, rotted steaks
killing and saving, more or less at random,
beetles, roaches, flies,
writing illegible puzzles
dead fish crammed in your ceiling

***

You always wanted *me* to be *your* mother
now you do it by supposed accident
you dare to call me your mother
I who am merely your irresponsible daughter
without shame you exhibit your toothless face

blindness and helplessness
selfishness memory loss
stinking incontinence
whether I wish or not
it is you, isn't it
I must cherish
mama
maya
even if winter sleet assaults the windows
like urine, hisses *too late, too late*
I myself must decide it's not too late.

    ***

Mom, reach into
your barrel of scum-coated blessings.
Find me one.

THE YEARNING

Not until the lower world
was made perfect was the other world also made
perfect . . . and it is thus the yearning from below
which brings about the completion above.

—THE ZOHAR

and so I am reading the zohar
and they are so splendid these old rabbis in their splendor
and their words are blazing light sparks gushing springs
and their hopes are palaces pomegranate trees perfumes ascending

glorious
but as for me
their gates stand closed
fastened against me

what must I do outside here
shake the latches and wail, they are deaf
mount a lawsuit against them, they are expert lawyers
scratch my scabs go on a hunger strike

forget it they own the cameras, oh my beloved
how long before you tell them: let me in
tell them I am your bride

FROM PSALM

You have made everything wondrous after its kind
the x molecule hooks the y molecule

mountains rise with utmost gravity
snow upon their shoulders

a congress of crows circulates through the maize
its sheen brightens through a breezeless morning

the ribbed leaf a spot of scarlet floats
on the shivering creek

each single thing so excellent in form and action
whether by chance by excitement by intention

you draw along a dappled path the wren
to her nest, the fledglings cry, the lions flow

rhythmically toward the antelope, the butterfly
flicks linen wings, the galaxies

propagate light in boundless curves
past what exists as matter, as dust

you have done enough, engineer
how dare we ask you for justice

you who lay justice in the hands of Cain
you who lean on the crutches of Law

THEODICY: A DIALOGUE

The spot of black paint
in the gallon of white
makes it whiter

so the evil impulse
is part of you
for a reason

what reason

greater wilder holiness

    ***

So perhaps you want us to understand
it throbs also in you
like leavening

you want us to love that about you
even if you pray that your attribute of mercy
may overcome your attribute of wrath

you want us always to love the evil also
the death-wish also
the bread of hate

because we are your image
confess you prize
the cruel theater of it

    ***

it follows then
the love of suffering
the suffering of love
that too is a spectacle to you
or do you feel it too
God, do you
feel it too

CALL AND RESPONSE

The Mother: Please, *please*
I can't see well
reassure me with your touch

or a tender word
the shade of a wing
or just *one* jay feather

or a snail shell, please visit me
please call me, please listen
to my story

    ***

The Poet: And the rhododendrons arrive, and so
you've survived another winter
shaky through clotted retinas

slowly reduced to one or two chopped letters
at a time mother you have spent
a lifetime reading only

to learn what words do not accomplish
though when I phone
today you say

there was so much sun
you sat outside
The Mother: I could read again

    ***

you remind me you were a wild one
you used to beat up the boys on your block

you were teacher's pet, you won prizes for poetry
everyone said you had beautiful eyes

you tell your neighbor I am your moon and stars
you are upset the plumber stole your purse

so I drive over and find it
on the counter among the flies

OUR MOTHERS: A CORRESPONDENCE

for Toi Derricotte

I send you my whitehaired poems
you reply: *our small box of words*
if we were men we would call it a word-hoard
like the warriors and bards in Beowulf

if we were real men
we would strut not cringe
over our language
what would we do
if we were real women

feed the hunger
chew everything
use up the words in the box
before we die
leave nothing to rot

      ***

Mother you coldly continue
as if with curled lip *some women*
walk away over the ice
leave their old mothers
to the wolves
in times of poor fishing
or when we cannot
bear them on our backs
any further

the wolves pace
just outside the perimeter of firelight
we can hear them pant
we admire the muscled grace
of their grey bodies all night in motion

      ***

All poetry is, you say,

    an attempt
to name the disappearance
that got in the way——
and I rise from my chair thinking yes,

it's the goddess, let's face it——
when they chopped her groves down
nailed her shrines shut
forgot the words to her songs

when she stalked back to myth
we lost something worth having
the men did it but the women
co-operated as usual

then there were ages
when stones dropped from walls
cities disappeared from the light of heaven
scattered buried

some statues remained
some painted figurines, some clay icons
snakes writhe in their fists
inside museum cases

we need to blame someone
we scream at our mothers
where is she? what have you
done with her?

THE SHEKHINAH AS MUTE

Our mothers tremble vibrate
hesitate at the edge of speech
as at an unmade bed, their mouths work, confused

our mothers helpless to tell us
She whom you seek sacrificed
her place before the throne

dived into the atomic structure
of matter and hides there
hair wings streaming

womb compassionate pitiless
eyes seeing to the ends of the universe
in which life struggles and delights in life

they cannot take our hands show us
how to take comfort in raisins and apples
break apart laughing spit seed

they cannot say *seek me*
they teach us cooking clothing craftiness
they tell us their own stories of power and shame

and even if it is she who speaks through their mouths
and has crawled through ten thousand wombs until this day
we cannot listen

their words fall like spilled face powder

NEVERTHELESS SHE MOVES

Let us study the gestures
as we find them in museums
and in our families

when her hands cup her breasts
she enjoys her sweet strength
sap ascends the oak

dancing she causes
the young to dance
and to kiss

she may carry a weapon
a knife a gun a razor
she may wear a belt of skulls

when she discharges her anger in laughter
white lightning illuminates the horizon
from pole to pole

often she lays her hand over her eyes
like a secretary leaving
an office building at evening

cradling that infant boy
sitting him on her lap
smoothing the folds of her dress: this means pity

arms crossed: this signifies judgment

BRURIAH

My ancestress
the one woman
who speaks in Talmud
an actual historical person
they say you learned
three hundred precepts from three hundred rabbis
in a single day a miraculous feat
they say when your twin sons died
you forestalled the grief of your husband
the great Rabbi Meir
saying: if someone lend me two jewels
then require them of me
what should I do
he said: return them
then you showed him the dead boys
and when your house was robbed
your husband wished to curse the thieves
so that they would die but you said
it would be better to pray
for their repentance
and they say once when Rabbi Eleazer
the conservative
met you on the road and
asked directions of you
you replied to him ironically:
should you not use fewer words
when speaking to a woman

five hundred years after your death
the sage Rashi relates a tale
that your husband cited a tractate
saying "women are light-minded"
that you denied this
that he set his student to seduce you
that you resisted then succumbed
and hanged yourself
let me beg to doubt this
the Romans liked such tales
Dido immolates herself for love

Lucrece stabs herself for shame
of such deeds the nations create high art
but what kind of story is this for Jews
why didn't your husband hang himself
for shame

my friend Jane visits Tiberias
the grave of Meir is a magnet
for pilgrims but
where is the grave of Bruriah
she wanders streets puzzled
no citizen can tell her where
you lie rather they seem appalled
or angry at the query
nobody has a clue
Bruriah my ancestress
how when you taught Torah
your words rang like a harp
such a clear mind you had
such a bright soul

THE VOLCANO BREATHES

coughs   coughs up

        *****

if the subconscious is a *geniza*   like Cairo synagogue   piled attic
        twelve jars a shepherd finds in a cave   papyrus crumbs

repository [place of repose   in which to put/ push/ press/ repress

        freeze   her moist red   disturbed
        rose   her terebinth   grove misremembered but

                    can't throw anything away
                        holy holy holy
                holy god holy name holy demon same

the mind can't
throw anything holy away
let it stay let it be she   let it wait

        in the collective memory   the denial of memory   let it wait

the delusion is that these atoms are inanimate [inaccurate]
        can you carbondate them   can   energy bits blister
decay hate, ooze heat,   through   open cracked lips smoke

        *****

oh god
yours and ours
it hurts

pain is the pressure of what attempts to be ex-
pressed and cannot be, oh shit, oh baby

            anguished impression is pressure to

she told them at the lecture the naked [failures] fathers
    what do you guess your pain and suffering mean
[she looked from the podium] looked round the room they were seated pretending
    no no pain no suffering
      not me insisted their eyebrows not my face I am
        a commercial for normal/eyes away
            only   a few lashes flickered

*****

dry crust in quiet flame ready now
    your labor pains persist indefinite exacerbate until
oh dear god, maybe never [fear is your driver, your doctor]

        oh god, yours and ours, how they hurt so
          bring forth your uterine self? by yourself? is it time's nick? [time present]
    she so buried so erased so unlawful so forgot so swallowed
        like wolf swallowing grandmother [the being
called] god the father swallowed god the mother,
      the process required [generations] millennia
      you swallowed her down the hatch

meanwhile in the text she kicks watch that

    to "raise the sparks" is   metaphor is   imagination is!
    to speak the unspoken   unspeakable   grassy stems cut asphalt
    lava through split stone, heaving water dividing
    razon, oh desire of god, your desire be done
let the waters break from the waters   fireflow rise

want to be a midwife to
  pull it out to dream

words of the mouth meditations of the heart

from the source the desire
is to flow without cease
I do have a heavy burden
and cannot wait to put it down

    ***

to put it down is forbidden

FROM **PSALM**

I am not lyric any more
I will not play the harp
for your pleasure

I will not make a joyful
noise to you neither
will I lament

for I know you drink
lamentation too
like wine

so I dully repeat
you hurt me
I hate you

I pull my eyes away from the hills
I will not kill for you
I will never love you again

unless you ask me

I DECIDE TO CALL YOU "BEING"

A word with two contradictory
meanings   someone to wipe the blood
and dirty tears away through boundless love

someone able   to punish listen wrestle
like a person but
larger

the other meaning   *ein sof*
be- ing in the sense of pure existence   remote
abstraction more impersonal than zero

you exquisite
joke   you paradigm paradox
you absent presence   you good evil   shredding the eye

so that it can become a door
you are inexplicable   like a *koan*
running uphill barefoot
blowing   the door down

    you complete nothing

    you perfect nothing

    ***

everyone asks   are you the father or the king
or the mother or the snake   but to me
you are the hope of my heart
you are the quarrel in my art

you are the tangled quarrel in my art
like a married pair who will go to their graves
carrying resentments like suitcases of foreign coins

you are the sex in my art
whatever wants to faint under long kisses, whatever grapples
flesh to flesh, the nipple that reaches, the tongue that spills

SEASONAL

when the full sun is on me this way
I itch and am satisfied

I take it in like a thirsty man
drinking from his garden hose

I take it in like a serene woman
receiving a man, and then when the golden leaves

rush past me sometimes I jubilate
like Abraham I am here for this I came

like Isaac I laugh trembling
well at least I am alive

and like Jacob I think in the spirit world they can never
experience pleasure the way flesh can

the body making love
the body nursing a child

the body fighting
playing basketball

even when it sickens
nursing its lesions

it struggles to stay
it clings to its bars

everything else is theology and folly

　　　***

Just now coming downstairs after returning some books to a shelf and reading
　　a few pages of a friend's book, his piece on Jacob's wrestling, I was flooded
　　with love for this friend, and in my happiness halfway down the stairs I
　　thought to glance at my interior—there, very faintly, was the claw of the
　　shekhinah, pinching; there too was her dark smile.

***

when she comes it will not be from heaven, it will be up from the cunts and
    breasts

it will be from our insane sad fecund obscure mothers

it will be from our fat scrawny pious wild ancestresses their claws

their fur and their rags

INTERLUDE: THE AVENUE OF THE AMERICAS

Above the tongues of taxicabs, the horns and buyers
the teeth of buildings grin at each other, the institutions
of media medicine publishing fashion

know how to
bite through human flesh
like hinged aluminum traps chopping the necks

of beavers, or like logging rigs, those saws
that go through a five hundred year old
redwood in about five minutes

take out a thousand acres
of virgin Oregon forest
annually because loggers need jobs

intellectuals need the special sections
of the New York Times stacked
on driveways

each rosy dawn, the Japanese need
the sawdust these pines and spruces
finally get ground into

everybody needs what they can get
and more. Yesterday walking
between fifty-third and fifty-second

on the Avenue of the Americas at twilight on my way
to a good restaurant with good friends I passed
three beggars. Wrapped in plastic. Why not say

beggars?
Why invent novelty phrases like "the homeless"
as if our situation were modern and special

instead of ancient and normal,
the problem of greed and selfishness?
The beggars turned toward me

I put money in the woman's cup
though I didn't like her facial sores
her drowned eyes bobbed to the surface

as if they believed for a second
something new was about to happen
but nothing was

so the eyes sank rapidly back
like crabs into sand, and sorrow
pressed into me like a hot iron

after which I hurried through the hurrying crowd
sky overhead primrose and lilac, skyscrapers
uncanny mirrors filled with cloud bouquets

to overtake my friends who had strolled ahead
chatting so as not to be embarrassed
by the sight of charity

the bad odor of need

MEMORY

I wanted to forget that I drank your milk
I wanted to uncurl your grip
and forget your sour smell

your voice pursued me into the tunnel
I ran splashing through puddles
it grew darker

I am afraid of rats and of darkness in strange places
the echo of gongs faded
I was in this concrete pebbly tube

finally it was completely dark
and so dank no breeze
no glimmer even of steel track

but the odor of mud
old snakeskins
hair

ABOUT TO SELL YOUR HOUSE

Yard overrun with raspberries
canes across the front walk
I fill two quart containers

with plump red berries
eating as I go
scratches inscribe my arms

I have hired someone to cut it all down
after you leave so this is the last crop
the fruit delightfully tender to the fingers

to the tongue deliciously sweet and tart
you would like me to eat it all
leave nothing for the neighbors

I am your child
you want to do something for me
mother, I am sixty-two

at last able to say the sentence
I love you—I say it
before getting into the car

REWIND

in the communal dining room
many of the residents scream

one woman repeats *I'm good, I'm good*
many sit and say nothing at all

you write a poem calling them *wounded animals*
we move you to a better wing

you claim someone has stolen your bathing suit
you tell people you love them

you sit with your ear to the cassette player
listening to a biography of Eleanor Roosevelt

when you came you had forgotten how to cook
you were living on saltines

my mother my queen
now you gain weight

here is the photo of you dancing
that was in the newspaper

I saved your writing even the scraps
I saved the letters praising you as a teacher

today you have wet yourself you have soiled your underpants
I embrace you when I arrive and when I leave

PHYSICAL EXAMINATION

you sit on the examination table
white hair flying
telling your tale

I sit on the leatherette and chrome chair
over your shoulder I look at the degrees
the aluminum shelves

the kindly doctor moves his hand
you remove your cotton blouse
lay it aside you wear no brassiere

you reveal your breasts
with their brown aureolas
my mouth waters

MEMORY

first dream I remember
maybe I was three
wearing a little coat
you were pushing a baby carriage
down the block away from me
you were running
my mother my queen
I was trying to catch you

No Heaven (2005)

*

Imagine there's no heaven,
It's easy if you try,
No hell below us,
Above us only sky,
Imagine all the people
Living . . .

—JOHN LENNON

VOCATION

To play among the words like one of them,
Lit from within—others can see it,
Never oneself—

She slips like a cat through traffic,
a girl alone downtown
for the first time, subwayfare in her purse,

fear of losing it
clamping her chest,
wind whipping tears from her eyes,

fried grease and gasoline in her nose, shoes and
jewelry in shopwindows, a needle
of freedom stitching her scalp—

though she dreads the allergy shot at the clinic
she feels herself getting brave.
Now it begins to snow on Central Park South

and a flight of pigeons
whirs up from a small pile of junk in the gutter
grey, violet, green, a predatory shimmer.

The marquee of the Paris Theater
looks at the rapturous child
through downcast lashes, condescendingly.

I watch her over a distance of fifty years.
I see how small she is in her thin coat.
I offer a necklace of tears, orgasms, words.

BIRDCALL

for Elizabeth Bishop

Tuwee, calls a bird near the house,
tuwee, cries another, downhill in the woods.
No wind, early September, beeches and pines,

sumac aflame, tuwee, tuwee, a question and a faint
but definite response, tuwee, tuwee, as if engaged
in a conversation expected to continue all afternoon,

Where is?—I'm here?—an upward inflection in
query and in response, a genetic libretto rehearsed
tens of thousands of years beginning to leave its indelible trace,

clawprint of language, ritual, dense winged seed,
or as if someone were slowly buttoning a shirt.
I am happy to lie in the grass and listen, as if at the dawn of reason,

to the clear communal command
that is flinging creaturely will into existence,
designing itself to desire survival,

liberty, companionship,
then the bird near me, *my* bird, stops inquiring, while the other
off in the woods continues calling faintly, but with that upward

inflection, I'm here, I'm here,
I'm here, here, the call opens a path through boughs still clothed
by foliage, until it sounds like entreaty, like anxiety, like life

imitating the pivotal move of Whitman's "Out of the Cradle,"
where the lovebird's futile song to its absent mate teaches the child
death, which the ocean also whispers—

Death, death, death, it softly whispers,
like an old crone bending aside over a cradle, Whitman says,
or like the teapot in Elizabeth Bishop's grandmother's kitchen,

here at one end of the chain of being,
that whistles a song of presence and departure,
creating comfort but also calling for tears.

PICKUP

It is all about speed and flexibility, about speed
and flexibility and teamwork and accuracy. We move
like neurons charging in your head, man,

choreography from the ground up,
meanwhile smelling the hot asphalt and exhaust,
the chain link fence around the playground spinning

past the corner of our eye, with the traffic and storefronts,
what the ball feels like in our hands, hard, pebbled, orange
and black, what the dribble feels like,

the sound and pound, the sort of lope we adopt
getting on and off the court, the way somebody looks
when he starts to play, his face and his sneakers, it's all part of it.

When we swivel it is a whiplash, when we pass it is a cannonball,
when we leap, we hang in the air like Nijinsky taking a nap,
when the ball goes in we slap each others' shoulders and butts

then turn like a flock of barn swallows, you know our ancestors
were farmers, they had barns, they watched the birds
flying around in formation at sunset,

or a school of fish, you know the way fish dart
in unison, the way the tempo changes and they just bat off,
you can't begin to guess how they do it. You could say

we slosh like waves in a bathtub, back and forth,
and when we dunk one it feels good, but
the way we play it, there are no pauses in this game.

LIKING IT

Some men like it if the woman can't tell
whether it's a gun she has in her mouth
or a prick.

Some women believe the shallow razor slashes
their lovers make on their necks
(underneath the long

elliptically tangled hair) and chest
are like a secret engagement dramatized by a real
diamond, to be proud of

but not reveal. He's her high school
mathematics teacher, and she does it to him, too,
because after the vodka comes the need to punish

their sinful bodies, she thinks about it all week,
bright red released in lines like devil's writing coming out,
the sharing of blood, the licking, the cleansing

of wounds, and how perfectly painful that is,
cuts even hiss from the alcohol swab, it's like acid,
and the candles in the living room dance like they're alive,

like hellfire, you can't imagine
the discipline required. The purity
of self-loathing needed to cut the man

you love—what do her parents understand about love,
she wonders, her poor parents not guessing
what her arms look like under her sleeves:

white nicks, white nicks, white crucifixes,
sharp little mouse tracks up and down. Some men
like you to wear a religious medal

when you fuck, some women
like the man to cry and beg forgiveness.

CROSSTOWN

Back in New York I grab a taxi at Port Authority,
a young Jamaican guy, then a big Af-Am guy in
a monster silver SUV tries to cut him off but he dashes
round in front like a fox and then can't move
so we're sitting in the traffic people leaning
on their horns all around us and the big guy comes
out and starts threatening my driver —*I'm just out
of jail.* —*So go back to jail.* No love lost it happens
all the time, *They think they are tough and we are
nothing, we think they are worse than nothing.*
He's been driving two years saving to go to school
to catch up on his computer design skills, the wife
got impatient and cheated on him, he still sees his
little daughter who is so pretty and smart she can
read at the age of four. He'd like to be a better
Christian but working this job he gets in situations
where he uses bad language. Next day another
cabbie this one older we talk about Iraq and about power
I say we are seeing the defects of democracy
He says he doesn't believe in democracy democracy
Is for the rich.

Went to Sheila's, we walked on Riverside Drive as
the sun was setting bathing the high limbs of the elms
coral, the trunks sinking into darkness, we were
happy together and other walkers also looked happy
trees tranquilly surviving blight seemed fine
a man passed us with a poodle so elegant it looked
like a model on a runway.

Small kid on the crosstown bus, a high clear voice:
If you kick somebody, people won't be your friend.
Woman next to me carries a large flat manila envelope
her makeup is violent her middle aged hair is lacquered
her coat olive green embroidered cashmere expensive
I think art? photography? then I see the envelope says
X-rays, so it's cancer.

MAY RAIN, PRINCETON

Green, green, the maples preen themselves
in my back yard, their moist cells plumping up
like lips of freshman girls before a dance,

the bird feeders need daily refilling, the hot
azaleas enhance their orange and fuchsia tints,
the rhododendrons puckered dryly inside

their big buds have begun to force themselves out,
apple blossoms lie in silent pools
at the feet of their trunks. All afternoon

relentless pouring rain soaks the ground,
beats the roofs, rat-tat,
races down the gutters.

I imagine it falling into the Hudson River
around the scows and barges. I imagine it
splashing the yellow slickers of road crews.

I pretend that I am farms and towns stretched out
the breadth of New Jersey and Pennsylvania
flat on my back looking up at a gray sky.

The grays shift, it must be windy up there,
I feel the rain batter me, how good it is, cleansing
the air, pocking my skin—

good, good, like sex after childbirth
when the body is keen
for pleasure again

RUNNING OUT THE CLOCK

for JPO

When we started living together we used to sit at a wooden table
side by side studying, touching each other between the legs,
remember, and in a sense we have gone on doing that.

We carry each other's minds everywhere for safekeeping,
our bodies bear traces of each other's bodies,
surface and depth, when you are absent I sleep on your side of the bed.

You made me laugh, I made you be serious, we taught each other
Whatsoever thy hand findeth to do, do it with thy might
and many other pieces of wisdom,

Thereby hung a tale, our tales, our tails, we worked our asses off
and played as hard as we could, not to waste the time that on earth
was given us, to live as our parents living and dead would approve,

to raise the children healthy and smart, and good and free,
to earn respect and love, though it is not polite to say it,
as much love as we could possibly—

Arriving at what should be the age of wisdom we keep very busy,
you say what we're doing is running out the clock
as if we could stop the other team from beating us,

or erase our mistakes. I say I feel the undertow,
some water still pushing in, breaking in a lively froth, but also
the seductive pull outward, downward, not especially cold or frightening,

more a call from afar, *Let go, little boat, let go, you can swim,*
whatever else we're doing, wherever we are, we are having this conversation—
after living so many years with the din of duty and of ego

if it is time to give them a rest, we wonder what will follow.
We are almost ready. Whether we sit at table or lie warmly in bed,
what we feel in our old bones is a little afraid,

a little set for adventure, getting ready to go.

THE SPEECH OF THE CREATURE

for Abigail

The night before you were born
I was sitting on a Berkeley floor drinking wine,
playing a game of Scrabble with the ones
who soon were going to be your parents
and losing badly, but before I went to bed
I told them to wake me if anything happened.

In the morning the March light woke me
flying through the eucalyptus
and the square windowpanes onto my quilt
and onto the varnished hardwood floor.
It was quiet in the house. Not a sound.
Out the window a cat was strolling the sidewalk.

The other bedroom was empty, also full of sunlight
and dancing dust, the furniture stood quietly
amid this emptiness that cannot be described,
it is so full of loss and of great space together,
pain and happiness together. While I waited for the call
from the hospital, you were leaving your tight wet world

forever, and as you know, a young woman scientist
and a young policy wonk—two serious people
who had lived whole lives without you,
did problem sets, read books, played ultimate frisbee—
were metamorphosing into your mom and dad.
Soon they were confused and new,
excited as if they had twinned themselves or something,
the way you're a different person with the dolls
that are your children, except they didn't want to boss you—
to them you were like ice cream,
to them you were the most precious pearl,
you were like the wildest magic in Harry Potter.

The third night of your life
when you couldn't sleep, I walked you for an hour
bouncing your small weight on my shoulder
sniffing your fragrant scalp, feeling where your
skimpy bottom was, your slender feet, your limp back
inside the yellow blanket like a puppy.

They played Beatles and Mozart your first week,
stubble grew on your father's chin,
your mother's breasts were huge and leaky,
you were the size of a large cat
and they cherished you so much it made me cry,
wishing every child born on the planet could have what

you have. There was a sink full of dishes I was washing.
Swaying with exhaustion your sweet dad was keeping me company.
Suddenly he frowned and said, *If anybody touches my daughter,*
I'll kill him. Both our jaws dropped, both of us laughed
at what came out of his mouth,
the speech of the creature.

MID-FEBRUARY

for Maxine Kumin

The mare rears, she has almost thrown her rider.
It's the thaw, it's the scent of spring,
the animals know it before we do.
While the lot of us shiver and fret
over the ozone layer and the whale,
incorrigibly peering forward and backward
in the manner of our species,
New Hampshire is a patient who seems to heal,
left to herself. See how she kicks at her blanket.

Inside here, the windows are steaming up
but a path runs through the woods,
half dirty snow, half mud
with the stones sticking through
and the snapped branches lying across, the ones
that were ready to die
and gave themselves to the wind.
Friend, it's a day for a walk.
Are we going to walk it?

CARAVAGGIO: THE PAINTING OF FORCE AND VIOLENCE

I

Abraham's thumb digs into Isaac's jaw.
Like all Caravaggio's victims Isaac howls.
Of course he is terrified,
the teeth show, the eyes bug out, pushed
into our faces inviting us to see
what it must mean to be obsessed and shameless.

Surprise is part of it, a father's
kitchen knife at our peachy throat, the father's
forearm restrained by the angel who has
hastily but firmly appeared on the canvas' left margin.

Abraham has forced his head round, looks annoyed
at the interruption, as if he might shake off the hand's pressure
in another instant, and on stage right
the profile of a comically stupid white goat,
almost more pasted than painted,
peers curiously at the entire scene—

This is a test—are you the boy, or the vigorous
old father, or the well bred angel, or the goat?

Do you place yourself in the hands of the living God?

II

The inner life holds no interest
for an art not of silence but clamor

The man is a gambler a lecher a drunkard a brawler
a man without delicacy who has "ruined the art of painting..."
"Works for a fortnight then enjoys himself for a month..."
Flaunting a vulgar unheroic Lombard realism
contemporary to Galileo and a world of solid objects
the human figure a physical object possessing weight
solidity balance and surface areas
no more difficult to paint, he boasts, than fruit or flowers.

His unseductive madonnas physical as his cheeky delicious
catamite boys,
his shadows like a fist
his light wielded like a shovel
large, arbitrary and inexplicable
the dirty feet of his peasants in the foreground
grey-pink, it is always a question of the truth
truth is always a question of force
to paint the hundred variations of force
the world requires an ignobly modern man
a quick man with a sword
a man who despises Plato.

III

As a chemist experiments patiently combining
materials and recording each effect
so he explores violence and forces
himself into each position out of nothing
but hot fascination, cold skill
a devilish indifference to all
but the unresolved tensions of any act
immediately prior to a final result
so that Judith performs her job of sawing
Holofernes' head off with a look of disgust and insult
on her housewife's countenance, her aproned upper
body pulled backward, her arms the arms
of a competent butcher;
the creased crone on our far right, however,
strains maliciously forward. *Do it, don't faint
now, young woman, do it! Kill the pig,*
urges her mean profile, unlike the goat's,
and the drunken general is twisting
his half decapitated self around to try and tell,
Che diavolo, what is happening to him—
Only the blood is unreal
leaving his neck not in spurts but stripes, like paint.

IV

When the giant's head is removed and the body nowhere in sight
when the victor suspends it in air by its own black greasy hair

still the image conveys no repose, no triumph or calm or ease,
for see how the youth's compressed lips are hardly at rest,

how his foreshortened arm has already begun to ache
so his shoulder will tire soon, he will set the gross head down,

how Goliath's opened mouth has not yet begun to drip
saliva, nor stunned eyes to admit their loss.

Behold through the broken brow how self repents its past
while David regards the horror his future holds.

***

The Sacrifice of Isaac, Uffizi Gallery, Florence
Judith Beheading Holofernes, National Gallery of Ancient Art, Rome
David with the Head of Goliath, Borghese Gallery, Rome

THE KISS OF JUDAS

Among many, one panel:
perhaps it catches the eye
due to its symmetry
or its subject, betrayal.

Giotto is simple.
What does "simple" mean?
Soldiers, torches, a friendship,
money, a kiss.

Two profiles: one looks upward,
lips protrude with intention,
brow slightly frowns.
And one receptive, brunette,

eyes almost Byzantine,
grave if not solemn,
his neck remains bare
to show absence of fear.

Judas wears a cloak
to reveal that he's hidden.
His embrace also hides
the other man's body.

Could Judas wish to become
joined with his Lord's body?
Giotto has painted him
like almost everyone else

in the Scrovegni Chapel,
slightly rounded, short,
not too far from being
a dog or a bird.

Isn't it hard, though, to leave?
Pope Leo liked them. We too,
those tender Giotto blues,
those rose tints, those ash-greens.

We were never in a church
more comforting than this one.
Imagine if women's wombs
had paintings like this one.

All of us would be born
wise and good, then.

Scrovegni Chapel, Padua

REMBRANDT: WORK AND LOVE

Your coach leaps forward like an act of love
from pious Leiden to Amsterdam, where you eye
the action, bankers and beggars, wealth and art,
fishwives and Jews at market. Your puppy face
eager for the life of art is pink-and-green
with ambition, innocent of defeat.

Some early paintings hint a fear of defeat—
a mournful Tobit with little dog, the busywork
of Jesus healing, a blinded Samson, the supine chrome
corpse dissected by Dr. Tulp—but the amber eye
triumphs, guilders roll in, your rollicking face
prospers beneath helmets and plumes, as art

would have it, and what pleasure to make art
of "the humble, the rough, the decayed," the lame defeated
whose inner tenderness rises like cream to their faces.
Or is it your own tenderness? What makes you eye
cottage and marble hall with equal love?
What presses you to draw from shadows a light

of something half divine, as it were gold
undimmable in a plowman's purse? and the art
to make *line,* that poorest mark, thoughtfully work
through flesh like God's compassion, etching defeat
like "the greatest inward emotion" a clear eye
can absorb? Then the theater of *Nightwatch.* Then you face

Saskia's death, creditors, the paintbrush slows, your face
grows plump but humble, ruddiness gone brown
as a muddy millstream, bankrupt, bags for eyes.
Old-fashioned for the times, your darkened art
makes Hendrickje a fat Bathsheba, denies defeat,
prepares a copperplate. Now what's left to love?

A window, a studio, a man in a smock at work.
Wearied, stubborn, finally I see in your face
The simple truth: the identity of triumph and defeat,
pride and humility, profit and loss. Through the black
crosshatch as you gaze outward from the art-
work you work on, here are your deathless eyes

shadowed by trouble, fortified by love,
looking me in the eye, helping me face
bravely my own short art and long defeat.

COSI FAN TUTTE: OF DESIRE AND DELIGHT

I   1761–1769

I might here take the opportunity of entertaining the public
with a story such as probably appears but once in a century,
and which in the domain of music has perhaps never yet
appeared in such a degree of the miraculous; I might
describe the wonderful genius of my son.

—LEOPOLD MOZART, "PRELIMINARY NOTICE"
TO THE SECOND EDITION OF HIS *VIOLINSCHULE*, 1769

Because Desire is a tomcat rubbing up
against a cook's leg, childhood a chemise
unlaced to suckle you, boyhood a room

in which your hands discover a complete
language to entertain yourself and them,
whose lexicon and syntax seemingly

lift through the wooden keys and offer touch
to fingertips you offer, let them come
to pleasure Papa too. What is it like

to reach and feel something reach in response,
desiring your desire to seek and find?
Between your lessons, Papa wants to know.

So! It is like dream-walking in a wood,
aware that you yourself create stately
beeches and oaks ahead as you proceed:

you sniff the air, a cuckoo chirps, a leaf
twirls silver, sunlight splashes between limbs,
an acorn drops, a gold ray strikes your shirt.

When you perceive you have produced that ray,
that oak and cuckoo, from the mind's brown seed,
it humbles you and crams you with a pride

you cannot then forget, cannot reveal
but in the language, gold, articulate,
already known for certain by your hands.

II   1789

—WOLFGANG MOZART TO MICHAEL PUCHBERG, 1788

Because Delight is a vessel upon a sea
smoothed by a halcyon and immortal breath,
whose passengers are young, do not know death,

do not lack coin, manners, or a bright
confidence in their own enlightenment,
who love like figures in a gallant dance,

rolling eyes upward if an elder prates
of God and duty, for do not the Estates
General proclaim the rights of man, and does not

civilization without discontent
prepare itself for fresh prosperity,
fresh liberty? Wolfgang, my lad, because

Munich and Prague delight to honor you
yet do not pay well, and because it's true
Papa is dead and life's a masquerade,

here's a libretto lets you trumpet what
fidelity and honor signify
among the crumbling privileged: suspend

your horns and strings from heaven's fulcrum like
a rope swing with a pretty woman on it
pushed by a pretty man in hose and wig

who is untroubled by a father, who
need not beg florins from inferiors.
Let your drums beat and let your fiddles play

in strict obedience to the sacred laws
of gravity, levity, of auburn curls
and skyblue slippers on the buxom girl

who swings while singing to enchant her friend,
Architecture is frozen music, and
Music itself a palace of melting ice.

SCHUMANN, OP. 16: THE GREATER HAPPINESS

On the stage Robert Schumann is getting drunk

with tempestuous love. You remember what it is to listen to passionate
nineteenth century music, a clamor of argument and struggle
invoking the old gods, thunderbolt and hurricane,
at the moment of their dying, and here in the lightning
is Clara whose father forbids her to marry him.

The middleaged pianist plunges through the keys.

At first I sit back to savor the performance, then suddenly find myself
inside a glissando as inside a storm, flooded and windswept,
then sense on my face an expression of my shy dead father's,
a twitch of ironic rue at the eyebrow, and presently I feel him
look through my eyes like sea-cave openings, bone binoculars.

The pianist pours his strength into Robert's ferocity.
Somewhere under the hurricane a sea-turtle rows through silence.

Thunder sings, fleecy skies shine, and my father can see
the music through my skull's apertures. He is happy for me
that in my life I can wallow in such music, not like his life.
Our family didn't do beauty, we did poverty, his soul aches with regret.
He too might have loved beauty but whatever you miss in this life you miss forever.

We sit together, my face awash in tears, pity for his jocular sneakers, his union card,
his eyes jealous when I went to college, my mother's pointless tirades,
my useless guilt. A girl who watches her father sink
under billows of anger must want to escape, but the truth
is I abandoned him. So I praise God

that the roads between the worlds are open again,
then he says to my soul, not in words, *Tell your mother I love her.*
And my soul is still more happy sitting in the velvet seat in the front orchestra
following the cadenza like an engine of tears, like a wet silence, arpeggios
trembling in every direction, *He loves her, he always loved her,* the wave

that overwhelms us is only a portion of ocean, what flooded my parents was just
thirty years of tragic human love, like between Robert and Clara,
like all passion when the gods are still alive,
and somewhere under the hurricane a sea-turtle rows through silence,
somewhere my father rocks asleep on the wave.

AN ALBUM OF CHINESE FAN PAINTINGS

It is late afternoon, the cherries bloom.
The master returns to his hillside pavilion
after a great absence.
Donkey trots him over bridge,
burdened servant follows with lantern,
a child runs up stone steps from the river
carrying two jars,
a dog comes forth to meet the master.

On a pole a banner
shows how the wind blows.
And this is all on silk.

Foreground cliffs, tongues of bristling pines
argue for nature's solidity, while a background
mountain half in mist argues against
this and many other illusions.
Tree-limbs, rocks, river, bridge, pavilion.
Browns, greens, washes and accents.
Tiny pink stipples—
cherry trees blooming in both the worlds.

*

Early fall, the maples auburn,
the cart driver crossing the ford
whistles to his bullocks.
Is he not a secret philosopher,
lover of the countryside,
of solitude and hard work,
such as holds a land together,
keeping peace among clans?

When nothing else is required of them
reeds doze, fish conceal themselves,
willows tremblingly wait to be noticed.
Space seeps back like a banished prince
to his own kingdom:
change, law, energy, presence.

*

The pathway of the sages climbs the mountain.
As it approaches heaven,
the mountain itself is tugged at the taproot
by the entry of the artisan.

Now the path pauses at a shelter
beneath hemlocks,
now rises through a drift
of moistened atmosphere.

To what should we compare the boundless forests?
They are like a swell of music
when the musicians are sober
and the patrons ecstatic.

The mountain is like a bell
that chimes quietly as the artisan
unbuttons his quilted vest, cocking his head,
setting down his bowl.

A WALKER IN THE CITY I

What you see is what you get,
an inventory of garbage lying loose—
the poor are always with us, but the rich
lurk behind one-way glass in limousines
and an entire class of attractive youth
increasingly able to make money
without actually working
increasingly are into arts and leisure.

There's power and there's glamor and there's grief,
that's what a city is for, it's why we come,
there's violence more or less unchanged
apart from a brief spike on nine-one-one.

The movies and TV are minting it.
Maybe the city should publish maps
showing the areas of greatest crime
for the benefit of the interested tourist
with special blue stars for locations
of especially famous crimes, the way in London
two shillings lets you follow the career
of Jack the Ripper with a little booklet.

Midtown East Side, here's where Robert Chambers
strangled his pretty girlfriend during sex
in Central Park. Up by the reservoir
someone from lower Harlem jumped and raped
and beat for kicks, get it, a woman jogger
into not death but coma. We thought it was
five boys, but that was wrong. Running between
a playground and a lake, Strawberry Fields,
some blackbirds in the shady sycamores
mark where across the street on 72nd
the Beatles fan Mark Chapman killed John Lennon.
Imagine there's no heaven, and imagine
The people living in a world of peace.
You have to take the A train to see where
Bernie Goetz pulled out his .44
and stopped the boy he thought another mugger

from sneering with his friends, from making fun.
They come on with their nasty stares, unlaced,
It's so hard to be white, to be a man,
when black kids don't respect you. Here's Howard Beach,
another white on black question of turf
and goodbye Yusef Hawkins. Here's where the woman guard
in the parking garage got herself shot
between bright eyes for being eyewitness
to some drug dealer's murder. Here a Bronx housewife
weary of scrubbing cracked linoleum
trying to clean her street of crack, lost it,
and the proud Haitian in his candy store the same,
as he wiped his hands on his apron,
and half a dozen children caught in crossfire
one steamy week in summer. *Mama, mama*
Ayudame, no puedo——Here's the house
where Joel Steinberg hit his little daughter
for pleasure, or for anger, breaking bone
after bone, yanking the soft blond curls
while the mom cowered in her druggie daze.
The case is special because he was a lawyer
and had a lot of money, otherwise it wouldn't count.
It wouldn't count. And in this very courtyard
of comfortable brick and stone
Kitty Genovese, mother of them all,
ushering in an era,
screamed, in 1960, being stabbed
several times in the chest by her old boyfriend,
Help me! Somebody help me!
None of the neighbors who heard that woman scream
for an entire hour called the police,
a sensible restraint, all things considered.
That was the sort of thing that shocked us then.

It is important to keep the selection of crimes
racially balanced and symmetrical
for tourist purposes, as the mayor says.
Right now everyone seems worried
about black people killing white people.

That's the disturbing thought if you are white,
though naturally most of the people killed
are men of color. There could be a key
at the map's bottom explaining what was what
if you are here on a self-guided tour.

Maybe the sponsors of the map could be
the NRA, and maybe they'd agree
to have an advertisement on the back,
like flower shops and banks in highschool yearbooks.
We'd need another color code to show
where most non-violent crimes have taken place,
Wall Street, City Hall, Police Headquarters, The Board
Of Education (Bored of Ed) and Columbia University.
Some people rob you with a knife
some with a fountain pen
some with an IBM.
And a map to show the areas
of crimes of omission?
Color the whole map red.
Color the city red.
Color it ghost white
for the death of compassion.

A VOICE AT THE RALLY

At fourteen I didn't want to be a demonstrator,
I wanted to be a sorority sister.
By the time I was eighteen
public opinion had changed,
first thing I read in the paper
was the obituaries.
I had a boyfriend in Nam
and let me tell you there were no *outside agitators*
bringing me out. I was there.
The day after Nixon called protestors bums
and the governor of Ohio said we were worse
than brownshirts and klansmen,
inciting guardsmen to see kids
like me
who just opposed the war
As *the most militant well-trained group ever*
Assembled in America,
Was the day it happened.
Four dead in Ohio, not just a song.
I have no forgiveness for the men who faced us
with fixed bayonets and hatred in their eyes.
It's twenty years and I'm still bitter.

Kent State, Ohio, May 1990

THE WINDOW, AT THE MOMENT OF FLAME

And all this while I have been playing with toys
a toy power station a toy automobile a house of blocks

and all this while far off in other lands
thousands and thousands, millions and millions—

you know—you see the pictures
women carrying their bony infants

men sobbing over graves
buildings sculpted by explosion—

earth wasted bare and rotten
and all this while I have been shopping, I have

been let us say free
and do they hate me for it

do they hate *me*

   NYC, September 11, 2001

POEM SIXTY YEARS AFTER AUSCHWITZ

for C. K. Williams

On a day of marching, the police in London
were bored and benign, not needing to keep order
for the million marching people were orderly.

Although they came from around the world,
they were mostly Englishmen and Englishwomen,
many carried signs saying "Make Tea Not War."

Horses stood motionless, questioned why they were not
allowed to move, and from time to time would shake
their glossy bodies impatiently. The marchers flowed over London

Bridge, flowed past Nelson remotely on his pillar
past Whitehall, past Green Park to Hyde Park, traffic was banned,
people were drops of water composing a river

and their signs and posters were a writing taken off the wall
and made into sails, what a beautiful clear cold day.
A day for sailing, a day for reading the signs.

I did not know life would inspire so many
to come out in its favor, patiently marching,
singing the occasional song. On the same day

in New York the marching permit was withheld
so the people and the police struggled,
forming whirlpools and dams, areas of dangerous turbulence,

some scowling mounted officers charged the crowd, let the
horses rear. There were other cities, Rome, Madrid, Mexico City
—and the weather was cold, or it was warm—

dozens of cities, people marching
like sands of the sea and stars of the sky,
or like stems of snowdrops nudging the frozen dirt

piled on their heads, unburying themselves
before it's officially springtime, here's a patch by the brick wall
next to our garage that I look up from my book to see,

glowing white and brave, a little afraid, a little aware
of the brevity of their visit here. It happens that
the book I'm reading is *Poetry After Auschwitz*

and I set it down after learning of a poem describing how
from a mass grave a fountain of blood spurting up
surprised even the officer in charge.

This is one of a thousand interesting stories the book tells,
for poems after the holocaust remember, or imagine,
how sick and sickening people can become,

and now I think we are writing the poems before the holocaust.
Is this not true? We are writing these poems with all our soul,
it's our writing, it's our wall.

February 2002, London and Cambridge

HUNGER

I

It was 1913 and there was no money.
She was born a runt who vomited everything,
so much poverty, such thin milk,
the doctor said to let her go in the dark
and have another child when there was money for food
but her mother persisted, insisted,
for months feeding and feeding
the skin on bones until she lived and grew,

but still remembers hunger, even now
shaking her soft white hair,
she remembers hunger and vomiting,
remembers seeing her mother approach with the bottle,
her desperate need to suck and be filled,
and at the same instant the grip of despair. And the force of will.

II

She remembers also the dresses her mother sewed her,
woolen, tucked, pleated, exceptional,
in dead European styles that made her ashamed
when she went to school, which insulted her mother,

but anyway, her mother never loved her
after that hard beginning. Fix your hair,
my grandma was still scolding in the wheelchair
whenever my poor mother visited

the Workman's Circle Home for the Aged.
Fix your hair, she would say, grimacing,
and reach to fix it, and my mom got rashes,
my mom got asthma before each visit.

III

They fired my father, they thought he was a Commie,
and it was still the Depression when I was born.
She remembers how she tied my arms and legs to the highchair
so that I wouldn't flail and she could get the spoon in
though she and my father were hungry.
She told that one to my school counselor,
boasting, and the counselor told me
to separate from my mother,
that she was crazy.

I wanted to be the best mother in the world,
she says in a voice like hoarded string.
That was what I wanted, but I failed,
here I freeze as always, and swallow my spit.
I failed, but I did my best.

As a girl she was a wild one, a *vilde chaia,*
she says into the little microphone
I hold for her as the casette whirs on.
She beat up a boy on her block who cheated at cards,
she refused to be tidy, she ran away from home.

We stand to go to the dining room, where because
the meal is free she will stuff herself as if
she were still that infant, she'll eat her own ice cream
and mine, she'll tell her neighbor that I
am her sun and moon and stars,
and before I leave she will hug me
as if we were lovers.

IV

And I too had my dreams of improvement and perfection.
I too hungered to give abundant life to my children.

FROM **ELEGY BEFORE THE WAR**

All the photographs are lies, she looks
normal in them, like other people,
not mad, not spilling lava,

her eyes are compelling as doe's eyes,
and she did not know this, and the worst of it is
she looks alive.

Putting the photos away, I also picture
how small and frightened she was in the hospice bed,
how light abandoned the hopeful eyes,

how the mouth gap with its gurgle from the sad
lungs made me feel like Moses, forced to see
God's backside from a cleft in the rock,

the mystery diminished not one grain,
the face and hands outside the cotton quilt
soft, horrible, fine—

how the jaw tightened then fell open
almost with a bang, the aide nodded,
everyone left, and then there was her silence,

a silence in which I stroked her moist forehead
then patted through the nightgown her belly and breasts.
O I loved her and this was her response—

I keep telling her to come back sometime.
Come back! I am not ready
to surrender hope.

    ***

My mother is dead two weeks

We were holding her hands and singing to her
when she let go. Very little pain, lucid
almost to the end, correcting

people's grammar
a week before
she died—

and we burned her and flew to Arizona
and the tanks roamed Ramallah and Nablus

I feel as if anything I have to say needs to be shaved down. I want my language
    to be like
the desert. My words and phrases to be like ocotillo, yucca, saguaro. Prickly.
    Thorny.
Able to collect moisture enough to survive extended drought.

The air I breathe is materially tropical, spiritually arid. These are dry times,
    orphan times,
Fear on the wind, anger in the soil. I cannot imagine an appealing future
For my species, that is born to violence.

Where is Shelley when we need him?
"An old, mad, blind, despised and dying king,
nobles, the dregs of their dull race,"

he begins a sonnet after the Manchester riots in which
British soldiers shot their fellow citizens dead.
Where is William Blake, is he burning

bright as the tiger in some grassy meadow of paradise,
does he beat a drum and shout "Holy holy holy
is the Lord God almighty," or, on alternate days,

"Exuberance is beauty," and where is Walt Whitman
and where is Ginsberg, genius of kindness?
I beg my mother come back sometime.

The root system of the saguaro
spreads shallowly underground as widely as
the cactus is high.

That of the ocatillo plunges.
The tanks roll, the missiles fly.

Greedy teeth blaze at the microphone.
They know where the oil is. They have plans, big plans
to connect the imperial dots.

I beg you awesome ones lift yourselves off the page
blow through us like a hot desert wind, as if we were trumpets
as if we were saxophones. Beat on our membranes hard

and let us be drums. Artillery
will always outshout us, testosterone explosions
are more thrilling than anything, chain reactions

brilliance between opposite poles accelerating
at the speed of hate, we do this
to you because

you did it to us first. Thrilling!
The bus explodes,

the shelled house collapses over the grandmother
and the gasping family, the tanks roll, the missiles fly

and perhaps the faster one dies,
the better.

    ***

But it does explain something.

I too look at the images

of cruel death in the newspaper and on the screen.
They taste good, I like them. You like them. They are their own
best advertisement. We like to shudder at them. We like to blame.

We bravely deplore. We enjoy a bit of fury.
The nearer we get to death, the more
we feel alive.

War, that great stimulant,
let us drink to it.
Let us join our friends, Israel and Palestine.

Our friends who have been seduced by it.

    ***

Now that it is spring I open the window at night

I lie awake in my cave, my well of night
pulsing like a bat
making inaudible orphan sounds

though the blinds stay down
soft air seeps in, a few cars
swish along the street

from the next house
where gloomy faded shingles fall like leaves
and bedsheets hang in the windows instead of drapes,

I hear the man's chronic unstoppable cough,
a poor man's cough, and the wife's hoarse voice
coaxing their dog.

Gypsy. Stop it. Come here.
Good girl, good girl.
I can work on

making music of that.

***

Friday night getting smashed in America

Ignorant violence that stuns the intelligence.
Dear animal inside us whom in other respects
we cherish, is it you?

Whitman and Blake inside us, celebrants of war equally with peace, is it you?
Descendants of Homer? Is it our stars? Is it our cold reason?
Is there a devil? Will somebody pass me that bourbon?

I think this impulse to destroy
this need for an enemy
has actually nothing to do with sex

it is simply a human characteristic
it has climbed the corporate ladder of the DNA
it is on the board of directors.

A joke in the Soviet Union went like this:
Under capitalism man is a wolf to man.
Under Communism it's just the opposite.

And there was that other one, about the economy:
we pretend to work, and they pretend to pay us.
Very funny, but because of low morale

the Russians have become ineffective soldiers
like the Italians and the French.
Long live the Italian and French armies!

Long live the citizens of Prague
whose twelfth century buildings stand
because a Czech will fight to the last

drop of ink! The trouble with America
is that her morale is still too high.
She needs to be a bit more depressed

before she starts behaving better.
The trouble with America
is she is a big bully

and a big coward,
also that she has no conscience,
not enough cynics, they are all in Europe.

Now let someone discreetly put on
The Stones or The Doors or better yet
Jimi doing the Star Spangled Banner

like a cry of absolutely
pained rage, a train jumping the tracks.
I like this party.

Perhaps you on the other hand like ignorant violence that stunts,
stints, stains, struts, standardizes, brutally strangles
the intelligence. Somebody must, why not you? Well,

here we need a few anti-American jokes.
What are we afraid of?
Where are the comedians

when we need them?
Tucked in their cages
like tame monkeys.

Where are the accountants?
Who will save us
from the mudslide of dollars?

***

She cried when she read Shakespeare

when I was young, she taught me not to hit or hate
anybody, she thought education was the answer, she said most people
were ignorant and superstitious but not us.

I miss her hugs though they were like clamps,
I miss her voice though she often mysteriously screamed
with rage at us all, the shopkeepers, the neighbors.

What drove her crazy, what wasted her beauty and intellect, was it America,
the *goldene medina* just a joke, land of bankers and lynch mobs
in her girlhood, land of brokers and bombs at her death,

hammer to which everything is a nail?

Or was it her pretty mother with the golden voice
and the golden hands that could sew anything
not loving her enough, the way she claimed?

Or was it a tricky couple of cells?
Little magicians sawing the woman in half?
My mother's secrets die with her,

the obsession with germs
the obsession with money
the anger at the world for cheating her.

Where did she go, my hopeful young mother,
my mother who promised we would overcome
the bosses and bigots? I want her. I want her

to come back and try again.

April 2002–February 2003

FIX

The puzzled ones, the Americans, go through their lives
buying what they are told to buy,
pursuing their love affairs with the automobile,

baseball and football, romance and beauty,
enthusiastic as trained seals, going into debt, struggling—
true believers in liberty, and also security,

and of course sex—cheating on each other
for the most part only a little, mostly avoiding violence
except at a vast blue distance, as between bombsight and earth,

or on the violent screen, which they adore.
Those who are not Americans think Americans are happy
because they are so filthy rich, but not so,

they are mostly puzzled and at a loss
as if someone stole the television and the cat
they'd like to believe in God, or something, and they do try.

You can see it in their white faces at the supermarket and the gas station
—not the immigrant faces, they know what they want,
not the blacks, whose faces are hurt and proud—

the white faces, lipsticked, shaven, we do try
to keep smiling, for when we're smiling, the whole world
smiles with us, but we feel we've lost

that loving feeling. Clouds ride by above us,
rivers flow, toilets work, traffic lights work, barring floods, fires
and earthquakes, houses and streets appear stable,

so what is it, this moon-shaped blankness?
What the hell is it? America is perplexed.
We would fix it if we knew what was broken.

DAFFODILS

for David Lehman

Ten thousand saw I at a glance
Tossing their heads in sprightly dance.

—WILLIAM WORDSWORTH

Going into hell so many times tears it
Which explains poetry.

—JACK SPICER

The day the war against Iraq begins
I'm photographing the yellow daffodils
with their outstretched arms and ruffled cups
blowing in the wind of Jesus Green

edging the lush grassy moving river
along with the swans and ducks
under a soft March Cambridge sky
embellishing the earth like a hand

starting to illustrate a children's book
where people in light clothes come out to play
to act out the journey of new life
with their lovers, friends, animals, and children

as down every stony backroad of history
they've always done in the peaceful springs
—which in a sense is also hell because
the daffodils do look as if they dance

and make some of us in the park want to dance
and breathe deeply and I know that
being able to eat and incorporate beauty like this
I am privileged and by that token can

taste pain, roll it on my tongue, it's good
the cruel wars are good the stupidity is good,
the primates hiding in their caves are very good,
they do their best, which explains poetry.

What explains poetry is that life is hard
but better than the alternatives,
the no and the nothing. Look at this light
and color, a splash of brilliant yellow

punctuating a bright green text, white swans
and mottled brown ducks floating quietly along
whole and alive, like an untorn language
that lacks nothing, that excludes

nothing. Period. Don't you think
it is our business to defend it
even the day our masters start a war?
To defend the day we see the daffodils?

The Book of Seventy (2009)

*

Barn burned down. Now we can see the moon.

—BASHO

FROM **APPROACHING SEVENTY**

I

Sit and watch the memory disappear
romance disappear the probability
of new adventures disappear

well isn't it beautiful
when the sun goes down
don't we all want to be where we can watch it

redden
sink to a spark
disappear

*

Your friend goes to Sri Lanka and works
for a human rights organization
in the middle of a civil war

where she too might be disappeared any time
and another friend goes to retreats
sits miserably waiting for ecstasy and ecstasy

actually comes, so many others
so many serial monogamists seeking love
some open doorway some wild furious breath

*

Please, I thought, when I first saw the paintings
De Kooning did when Alzheimer's had taken him
into its arms and he could do nothing

but paint, purely paint, transparent, please let me
make beauty like that, sometime, like an infant
that can only cry

and suckle, and shit, and sleep,
boneless, unaware, happy,
brush in hand no ego there he went

*

A field of cerise another of lime
a big curve slashes across canvas
then another and here it is the lucidity

each of us secretly longs for
as if everything belonging to the other world
that we forget at birth is finally flooding

back to the man like a cold hissing tide
combers unrolling while he waits on the shore
of the sandy canvas brush in hand it comes

*

So come on, gorgeous, get yourself over
to the shore with the sleeping gulls
—does the tide rise or doesn't it

and are you or are you not willing
to rise from sleep, yes, in the dark, and patiently
go outside and wait for it

and do you know what is meant by patience
do you know what is meant by going outside
do you know what is meant by the tide

III

Espresso bubbles, I shout
Breakfast in a minute up the stairs
he comes down robed, we have

coffee, toast, cherry tomatoes, cheese,
fish, juice, almond pastry, the *Herald*
Tribune then the long busy day then evening

in the tub after a smoke I remark
economics doesn't interest me
the three things I care about are individual

human lives, then art and beauty
then politics and cultural history and mythology
I'm thinking: apart from the personal stuff

on the other side of the tub my rational man
says truth then fun then honor, by honor he means
both reputation and doing what is right

head to foot we recline in the warm steam
while I remember a few summers ago
the mango tangy cool night air

that blew in through the bathroom window
as we stood in the tub looking out
side by side trying to locate the comet

with the double tail, ah there it was
off to northwest over the neighbors' charcoal trees
difficult to see, like the lightest pencil touch

INSOMNIA

But it's really fear you want to talk about
and cannot find the words
so you jeer at yourself

you call yourself a coward
you wake at 2 a.m. thinking *failure,*
fool, unable to sleep, *unable to sleep*

buzzing away on your mattress with two pillows
and a quilt, *they call them comforters,*
which implies that comfort can be bought

and paid for, to help with the fear, the failure
your two walnut chests of drawers snicker, the bookshelves mourn
the art on the walls pities you, the man himself beside you

asleep smelling like mushrooms and moss is a comfort
but never enough, never, the ceiling fixture lightless
velvet drapes hiding the window

traffic noises like a vicious animal
on the loose somewhere out there—
you brag to friends you won't mind death only dying

what a liar you are—
all the other fears, of rejection, of physical pain,
of losing your mind, of losing your eyes,

they are all part of *this!*
Pawprints of *this!* Hair snarls in your comb
the glowing clock the single light in the room

HONEY OF GENERATION

I am shy with them
since they became free

this one lily sleek dancer bass player art editor
actors and artists her colleagues and friends

this one lilac in her father's trade
a sharp astrophysicist with two daughters

of such brightness it makes me blink
this one hyacinth a singer carpenter bold rock climber

makes a living doing something with computing
of which I am ignorant

they are all so cool
they give me chills

then here am I
the blown peony

when they remember my failures and follies
committed in anger or pleasure will they forgive me

flesh of my flesh bone of my bone
going on going on

LATE WINTER RAIN

for Sallie

Sweet late winter rain
licks my study windows
while I meditate you come
a ghost a guest

plant yourself near my left eye
look at me bemusedly
sit across the small table at Main Street
the way you used to and order a vodka

I'm happy to see you
you reach over and lay your hand on mine
liver-spotted loose-skinned hand
direct lapis lazuli stare

Honey, you say in your old whiskey
and cigarette voice you had the good fortune
to retain when you stopped smoking and being a drunk
don't worry about a thing

being dead is okay, then you melt
into the rain

WEST FOURTH STREET

The sycamores are leafing out
on West Fourth Street and I am weirdly old
yet their pale iridescence pleases me

as I emerge from the subway into traffic
and trash and patchouli gusts—now that I can read
between the lines of my tangled life

pleasure frequently visits me—I have less
interfering with my gaze now
what I see I see clearly

and with less grievance and anger than before
and less desire: not that I have conquered these passions
they have worn themselves out

and if I smile admiring four Brazilian men
playing handball on a sunny concrete court
shouting in Portuguese

goatskin protecting their hands from the sting of the flying ball
their backs like sinewy roots, gold flashing on their necks
if I watch them samba with their shadows

torqued like my father fifty years ago
when sons of immigrant Jews
played fierce handball in Manhattan playgrounds

—if I think these men are the essence of the city
it is because of their beauty
since I have learned to be a fool for beauty

THE PLATEAU

The climb was long
and often dangerous,
there were recriminations,

stumblings, and yet
never did I desire another
for my companion on this path

so at last we have gained the plateau
the delicacy with which we attend
to one another's liberty is remarkable

our demons sleep in their caves
like angry children who have sobbed themselves
into exhaustion, while the grownups smile

you praise my writing my cooking my kindness
I admire your jokes your politics your photographs
and now shall I make a prediction?

someday one of us
will begin to die
to lean on the other

with horrible need
and passion, passion
will flow again

OUR DEAD FRIEND

Our dead friend used to say
when she reached menopause
the swamp cleared from her mind

the sun shone brightly
for the first time since girlhood
she could think clearly

Things were outlined as if in lights
a dog was a dog and a man
was only a man

     *

Imprisoned in the arms
of Eros you relax you blur
you have no will of your own

almost anything
can make you tingle with delight
music art nature kisses touch

the wetness the pulsing
every glance a sort
of soft bullet she said

     *

How true and what a fool
I made of myself
all those years

well we all did, you and I
honey we were like those lab mice
that will step on the pedal

that gives them those thrills
not eating not stopping
until they die

*

Now when I look at my body
under the spell of gravity
I have to laugh

Oh my god the way we all lined up
like a fleet of taxis at a red light
just waiting and racing our motors

what a joke sex is though without it
no avenue to paradise
no human glue

PERSEPHONE TO DEMETER

You up there on the surface
poor sad woman ratty old quilt

you understand nothing
of the rapture of liberty

no I am not afraid of the subway
or the smell of piss

or the ravings of the druggies
let them look up my skirt as I saunter past

the dead soldiers who killed each other revere me
the raped girls rush to kiss my hand

it was cool going down those iron stairs
then warm and with a breeze

with a faint tinge of smoke
or was it possibly gunpowder . . .

DEMETER TO PERSEPHONE

I watched you walking up out of that hole

All day it had been raining
in that field in Southern Italy

rain beating down making puddles in the mud
hissing down on rocks from a sky enraged

I waited and was patient
finally you emerged and were immediately soaked

you stared at me without love in your large eyes
that were filled with black sex and white powder

but this is what I expected and when I embraced you
Your firm little breasts against my amplitude

Get in the car I said
and then it was spring

GAIA REGARDS HER CHILDREN

Ingratitude after all I have done for them ingratitude
is the term that springs to mind

Yet I continue to generate
abundance which they continue to waste

they expect me to go on giving forever
they don't believe anything I say

with my wet green windy
hot mouth

LORD KRISHNA TO THE SUMMER HANDYMAN

Whenever you hammer I'm here inside your arm
which to me resembles a 'sixty-five Plymouth

seedy but comfortable. When like a boy
you go barefoot through the house, completely happy,

I'm the pine floor, the whitewashed
walls and the open windows, I'm also the spiders

and the rush of color outdoors,
I smell like one muddy thing after another.

Late afternoon you're tired, you need a beer
I'm a cold beer hitting your palate

I'm not particular. When
next fall your pretty wife

throws a final fit and walks out,
I'm her too.

BORN IN THE USA

Born in 1937 in the USA
not yet a war year though war was looming
along with its patent leather and bowtied photographers

When I say I feel like a rusty Dodge
I reveal my age my brand in an age of brands
here I am that depression era child

whose father took her yearly to Coney Island
where we ate Nathan's frankfurters
whirled madly in cars of remarkable lacquers

stood with the crowd sighed at the fireworks
at the end an American flag gleamed over the ocean
telling us it was time to head for the subways

damp sand blowing across the boardwalk
linoleum stained with juices and an oilcloth table at home
where we beat time and sang

Oh you can't scare me I'm sticking to the Union
for we believed a better world was coming
such and such my sources and my spring

for which I sink to my knees in gratitude
and dare you my fellow citizens
in the nation of money

I dare you to mock me

LAUNDRY

Just finished folding laundry. There's the news. A slender prisoner, ankles shackled, nude back and legs striped by a brown substance you might take for blood but which probably is feces, hair long, arms extended at shoulder level like a dancer or like Jesus, walks toward a soldier with rolled-up pants and a gun, posed legs akimbo in the tiled corridor. I cannot say from the image if the soldier is smiling, too few pixels to tell. Barely do the prisoner's elegant feet touch the floor. In another nude photograph a prisoner with shorter hair cowers against a wall while two dogs whose leashes are held by soldiers examine him. I cannot say from the photograph if the dogs are snarling or drooling. And in this one a girl soldier holds the leash, which leads to the neck of a prisoner lying on concrete.

Oil oozes a mile or two underground. Like sand, it was once alive.

In another photo the nude prisoners have been formed into a pyramid. They look like something in the back of a butcher shop. A stack of magnified calves' livers. Now the girl soldier leaning over a bleeding prisoner—are those dog bites— gives the thumbs' up sign and smiles her toothy Homecoming Queen smile. Oil oozes a mile or so underground. Atop it stands a palace of air conditioning. Somewhere in the green zone is a swimming pool for the officers, its water chemically purified. Stagnant waters are also good—for the flies. As is blood. A fly's life there would be prosperous. I put away the laundry. I put my nose in the laundry, it smells warm and well. My husband's underpants and undershirts I lay in his dresser drawer. In my dresser drawer go my underpants and t-shirts.

The correct word is not *prisoner*. The correct word is *detainee*.

Speaking of correctness, some other terms have lately come into play: *hooding, waterboarding, rendition*. The bleaching of the news. The rinsing and spinning. Some of the laundry items are not quite dry, a knit sweater of mine, a flannel of his. I hang them on plastic hangers in the bathroom. The bathroom is tiled in white, the tub is tourmaline. Above our twin sinks hangs a large flat mirror in which we are obliged to see ourselves each day, and on the opposite wall, that is to say behind us when we stand at the sink, a Rodin watercolor sketch depicts a semi-nude woman in some sort of peach diaphanous garment, seated, holding one pink knee in her hands, her shaven pubes showing, the lines at once easy, comfortable, and elegant. The correct word is *detainee*. The sweaters hang patiently. The mirror ponders a rebuke.

DEAR GOD

It used to be
I would fall to the floor and press my forehead to it
in moments of despair

I would say help me
help me

but listen
I am ok
though I just now found myself pressing my forehead
to the carpet of my stairs

about the waters in the flooded cities
poisoned by oilspill, chemicals, the dead
about the survivors forever traumatized
dear god
I am alive I am alive
help them

At the Revelation Restaurant (2010)

*

An incident here and there

—H. D., "THE WALLS DO NOT FALL"

THE BIRD

The sharp-clawed bird could never
have left that wound in your neck

unless it spotted you—from the sky—
out in the open, a moving dot

You got away that time
the wound is healing

no more wide open spaces
for you but my dear

no human
can hide from that bird forever

ISLA MUJERES

The first and final kisses are the best,
they carry secret meanings like pregnancies,
they attach themselves to your tongue.

In between you may encounter technique
without sincerity, or sincerity without technique,
or neither, or both. In sea, in bronze.

Fateful is the gull
who nests in your soul.
Fateful are her eggs.

We say this thing is merely sexy, this other thing is erotic.
It is the palm trees in the wind, the fronds
wildly caressing each other.

Thrashing and caressing.
Creating a hissing and a clicking sound
inside of the wind and the dirt.

LOVE I

Too late for mating season
what is the cardinal doing
all week flying between

the feeder outside my kitchen
and the hedge by the brick wall
where a female or is it a juvenile

waits with needy beak wide
yellow-pink inside—not cheeping but
vibrating its wings so fast

they blur like a hummingbird's
it's the same thing
girls do with their eyelashes

the adult male pecks some seed
for himself then gracefully swoops
to her low branch

and feeds her
gets some for himself
and feeds her again

all week this goes on
and I am almost stoned
just from watching

LOVE II (SUMMERTIME)

Somewhere between 116th St and Pennsylvania Station
the Broadway train rocking along and stopping

to let people off and on, then rocking and stopping again
they began to kiss in the way lovers do

when they want everyone to notice their bliss
and perhaps, even, to share some of it

so I thought it was appropriate to stare
I liked her turquoise tank top, her dangly earrings, his curls

but nobody else was staring, I couldn't think
why not, except an old black lady across from me

a big shopping bag between her knees
when we caught each other's eyes

we smiled a quick been-there-done-that
conspiratorial old lady smile,

while the subway lights flew by
and the month was deep July

LOVE III

In the ocean said the oceanographer
there is no place to hide
beluga whales protect each other
by traveling in a group

probably the instinct to save
any individual that seems to be sinking
as they do with babies and others in trouble
by lifting them from below into the air

is not species-specific so that when the young
diver began to choke thinking
now I will die she felt this irresistible force
almost like a machine push her upward

until she breached and breathed
rinsed by the sky
but the giant form dove and disappeared
into the immeasurable sea

those of her own species drew her up
peeled her suit off, wrapped towels around her
wondered why she cried and cried
since she had not died

LOVE IV

for JPO

Say it is a path through wilderness
   say it is the room where we undress

say it is a mountaintop, say it is a mound
   say it feels like crawling underground

say it is a lethal weapon taking a giant toll
   say it is a camera taking photos of the soul

say that it moves the sun and other stars
   or idly makes and breaks, and mends and mars

and will continue ruling us this way
   all of our lives, no matter what we say.

ARS POETICA: SEVEN POEMS

    Her throat tightens

Suspect says Jesus told him to stab.
Her throat tightens. Too sad—
pain at the beginning of all song.

Many a time, many a time her voice
disguises itself as silence
ultimately it opens her throat

    Breathe in, breathe out

What you fear to say
turns to poison in your body

it will kill you
one way or another

so breathe in reality
breathe out truth

if you can—if you can
manage to find words

Gear hangs

Gear hangs clashing from your belt
air pierces your lungs
your sweat
runs into your eyes

no hand free to wipe away the sting
you place the next wedge
drive it into the rock
slowly climb the next ten feet

The pull

The pull of the fish on the line
like the hard steady current of the river

and you pulling back equally steadily
in water to your waist

under a summer sun
that bakes the back of your neck

jigs of splashy light teasing the eye
delighting not distracting you

from the thing you are trying to catch
that is trying to flee

Strategy

When the wind is against you, run faster and keep your head down.
When there is a cross wind, run faster.

When there is a tail wind, fly.

The question of form

Builders having a lunch break
Fifth of May
sitting outside in the sun
not thinking about
the question of form

building goes up from
hole in ground big crane
steel girders, poured concrete,
elevator shafts, sheer glass walls, yah
finish your sandwich

You make it

—for others unseen and unborn
      —Muriel Rukeyser

For yourself   for the world
the world now   the world to come
brimming over with unborn
run by unborn
unborn gripping the wheel
a world imagined by your saints
your visionaries
the rich and the poor
eating the same vegetables

you make the story not for pay
for pity's sake
you vow to make it true
undiscovered truth maybe bitter
also gorgeous
your hands remembering cool clay
before there was speech
one hundred thousand years
that same cool clay   today

technology slings options like chickenfeed
what locale what style   you ring
fame's doorbell and you don't know

Is the story
tragic or humorous
or both or neither
could a movie be made of it
probably not
nonetheless
it is your life
it is the story
of your life

The Old Woman, the Tulip, and the Dog (2014)

*

A very important thing is not to make up your mind that you are any one thing.

—GERTRUDE STEIN

THE BLESSING OF THE OLD WOMAN, THE TULIP, AND THE DOG

To be blessed
said the old woman
is to live and work
so hard
God's love
washes right through you
like milk through a cow

To be blessed
said the dark red tulip
is to knock their eyes out
with the slug of lust
implied by
your up-ended
skirt

To be blessed
said the dog
is to have a pinch
of God
inside you
and all the other dogs
can smell it

DEER WALK UPON OUR MOUNTAINS

When they see me said the old woman
they stop where they are
and gaze into my eyes for as long
as I am willing to stand there
in the wind
at the edge of the forest

You are speaking of my mortal enemy
said the dark red tulip
they have eaten many of my family
they do not spare children
they are pests
beauty excuses nothing

Oh cried the dog
the very thought of them
thrills me to the bone
the chase as much as the capture
the scent weaving ahead of me like a flag
saliva spinning from my teeth

THE DRINK TRIPTYCH

Well what can I say
said the old woman
giggling a bit
a glass or three of wine was normal at dinner
but one also enjoyed martinis
gin and tonic to celebrate spring
in summer rum straight up or a margarita
sparkling champagne
for especially festive occasions

You see said the tulip
we who drink nothing but pure rainwater
remain awake and alert perhaps we shiver
and cannot but notice
the way you stumble getting home
after one of your evenings
scarcely able to find your keys
while we remain upright on the spine
of our stems our petals locked

My long pink tongue said the dog
is one of my best characteristics
so when I finish my porkchop bone
they put the bowl out
and I drink from it
slurp slurp lap lap
slurp slurp lap lap
making a great deal of noise
to show my appreciation

SONG

Some claim the origin of song
was a war cry
some say it was a rhyme
telling the farmers when to plant and reap
don't they know the first song was a lullaby
pulled from a mother's sleep
said the old woman

A significant
factor generating my delight in being
alive this springtime
is the birdsong
that like a sweeping mesh has captured me
like diamond rain I can't
hear it enough said the tulip

lifetime after lifetime
we surged up the hill
I and my dear brothers
thirsty for blood
uttering
our beautiful songs
said the dog

THE WIND THAT BLOWS THROUGH ME

I feel the hand of God inside my hand
when I write said the old woman
I am blown away like a hat
I swear God's needy hand is inside every atom
waving at us hoping we'll wave back

Sometimes I feel the presence
of the goddess inside me said the dark red tulip
and sometimes I see her
waltzing in the world around me
scarves flying though everything looks still

It doesn't matter whether you call the thing
God or goddess those are only words
said the dog panting after a run through the park
and a sprint after a squirrel
theology is bunk but the springtime wind is real

SOFTEN AND MELT

the man made me soften and melt
said the old woman

the bee made me shiver like a rag
said the dark red tulip

the bitch made me push
said the dog

APRIL

The optimists among us
taking heart because it is spring
skip along
attending their meetings
signing their email petitions
marching with their satiric signs
singing their give peace a chance songs
posting their rainbow twitters and blogs
believing in a better world
for no good reason
I envy them
said the old woman

The seasons go round they
go round and around
said the tulip
dancing among her friends
in their brown bed in the sun
in the April breeze
under a maple canopy
that was also dancing
only with greater motions
casting greater shadows
and the grass
hardly stirring

What a concerto
of good stinks said the dog
trotting along Riverside Drive
in the early spring afternoon
sniffing this way and that
how gratifying the violins of the river
the tubas of the traffic
the trombones
of the leafing elms with the legato
of my rivals' piss at their feet
and the leftover meat and grease
singing along in all the wastebaskets

IN EVERY LIFE

In every life there's a moment or two
when we disappear, the cruel wound
takes over, and then again
at times we are filled with trees
or with birds
or with polishing the furniture
said the old woman

I know what you mean said the tulip
about epiphanies
for instance a breezy April day
the approach of a butterfly
but as to the disappearing self
no
I have not yet experienced that

You are creating distinctions
that do not exist in nature
where "self" and "not-self" are like salt
in ocean, cloud in sky
oxygen in fire
said the philosophical dog
under the table scratching his balls

ANGER I: GRAY CEMENT

Neither my mugger
nor my rapist
nor the gypsy in Florence who cleverly stole my wallet
while I admired her daughter's baby
in front of Santa Maria Novella
a good professional job
they owed me nothing
but the smooth men who promised me and lied
the politicians who promised me and lied
should fry in hell and be smeared on toast
said the old woman

You admire me do you
coming and going the way you do
using your extra stem
tra la la the privileged lot of you
casting your gaze over the lot of us
approvingly but who are you to judge
merely because of my immobility
you imagine yourself so superior
crouch down
you are in my light
said the dark red tulip

They sold my brother said the dog
the new owners trained him
no meadow no tossed balls no sandy beach
hard palm short leash they made his poor wet nose
a killer's tool
taught him to track to threaten to snarl
whether in a train station or a grey cement prison
they yell *get him*
it excites them
they like
to watch my brother drool and attack

THE FEAR TRYPTICH

A rung above anxiety
and below dread
on the ladder of negative sensations
produced by adrenalin
said the old woman
once it meant something was coming to get you
today it means you recognize
your mind is slowly turning to mush

I wish I knew what they meant by it
said the tulip
I can feel it coming off them like steam
yet here I am and I am simply happy
my meaty bulb is fixed in the warm earth
happiness keeps rising through my stem
the sun shines in my face
what can be wrong

Again the man in the white coat
a very nice man said the dog
and they are stroking me
over and over on my belly
and gently pulling at my ears
the way I like
wait
stay away from me with that silver thing

THEY SPEAK OF RACE

Honey I am one gorgeous permanent wave
of dunebeige yellowgold coalblack European Asian
African force funneled through centuries
of ejaculating ancestors right here to me
said the impure old woman

Of course as the science of genetics informs us
we hybrids are the ones that survive
through the endless brutalities of storm and drought
and the rivalry of our peers
said the naturally selected red tulip

Any tribe keep doing the same
thing with the same folks
they gonna die out soon so procreate like me
with strangers go mix it up
mongrel is powerful said the dog

RIDICULOUS

This is ridiculous
said the literary old woman
nobody gives us any respect
the young in one another's arms
are talking on their iPhones
the politicians are lying through their teeth
and our husbands are watching the game

this is ridiculous
said the tulip
all those genetically altered blossoms
those stupid long-lived orchids
that are practically plastic
and those fancy designer grasses
getting more than market share

this is ridiculous
said the dog
now they not only have to walk me
they have to rush up after me with their
sanitary plastic bags
imposing their bourgeois values
on my spontaneous creativity

AWAKENING

It can take a lifetime
says the old woman

It can take a single deep kiss
says the red tulip

Time to take a nap
says the dog

I WANT TO LIVE

I want to live
said the old woman
like a flame in flight
sky cloudless visibility unlimited
looking down from a United
Airlines window gin and tonic in hand
at the green and golden graphics of agribusiness wheat
the action painting of the Rockies the Cartier bling
of a nocturnal city
knowing what I know
what everybody knows
about my country
the leeches
the worms
look I can still shed sparks
of pride at its unsurpassed beauty

I want to live
a life of passion
said the dark red tulip
you see how hot how velvety I am
come a little closer
do not close your eyes
in fear
of the moisture
in the depths of my well
do not casually turn away
here I am in the suburbs
not going anywhere but
look at me
I'm a flame too
and I will perish
like a flame

I want to live
where I can have it all
said the dog and that means
the Big Apple the stimulating
street life the nose-
enhancing fragrances
does it surprise you to know
my favorite is snow
though I also like
being able to scratch in the dirt
and having people
ask my owner
my name
it flatters my vanity
and does good things
for my owner's social life

THE SORROW TRYPTICH

The gift of tears
said the old woman
like the gift of laughter
is a kind of cleansing
a rinsing out
I discovered this as a child
when my grandfather died
I cried a lot
prayed for him each night
grew a little older
a little more free

You see me droop
said the dark red tulip
you see my violent redness
growing a little brown
a little dry
where I was moist
you see the hinges of my petals
subtly loosen
like old roof shingles
like a heavy flag taken down
and folded up while the day
is still bright the sun still shining

I try always to be obedient
to do the pleasing thing
in bed with them
I don't bounce around
I am quiet as can be
It's so nice lying between them
under their cotton quilt
they smell so good
said the dog
there was no reason to make me leave the room
or to have pushed the door until it clicked
honest to god I wish dogs could cry

ANGER II: THE RAPE

No cruelty is like the cruelty
one turns against oneself
after being raped
one feels covered in slime and shit
said the old woman grimly

This place used to be a park
now it is a parking lot ha ha
for which I am in the ornamental fringe
don't tell me I should get over it
said the tulip sourly

Definition of a bleeding heart—
you could not bear to look so you
crossed the street and did nothing to stop
the man on the corner with the stick
beating me said the dog belligerently

IN WAR TIME

Ah here you are at last
sorry about the guards
I hope they didn't give you much trouble
I was afraid you'd never make it
across the river before curfew
let me take your coats
said the old woman

thank you
how could we possibly pass up
such a sweet invitation
but let me tell you
said the tulip
when we reached the bridge we saw
the river was full of corpses

a dog too can be afraid
despite an appearance of ferocity
navigating unfamiliar streets
dodging unpredictable explosions
still one persists in one's errand
here we are said the dog
thank you I will keep my coat

PAW ON YOUR LAP

Remember the funniest place we ever made love
a pair of Economy seats on an overnight to London
we imagined nobody noticed... how hilarious
what a thing to remember for fifty years
said the old woman

Poured upward I'm a slender jadegreen tube
whose tip is swollen and hurting...
although I am half asleep barely a bud
let the wind touch me tenderly with its tongue
said the tulip

Under the table my nose nudges your shoe
toss the ball I return it increasingly moist
walk in the door I admire your crotch confess
your species too craves touch...paw on your lap
said the dog

BRIGHTNESS FALLS FROM THE AIR

Brightness falls from the air
said the old woman
like Bach's cello concerto
played by Pablo Casals
traveling the universe gently
like deep blue dust
I call it evening

Brightness falls from the air
said the dark red tulip
and when it does I lock
myself in the house
I draw the blinds
all night I breathe
my own suffocating perfume

Brightness falls from the air
said the dog
well so I use my brain
this happens all the time
If I go to sleep now
It will be bright again when I wake up
goodbye

Waiting for the Light (2017)

*

Everything is plundered, betrayed, sold,
Death's great black wing scrapes the air,
Misery gnaws to the bone.
Why then do we not despair?

**—ANNA AKHMATOVA,
TRANSLATED BY STANLEY KUNITZ WITH MAX HAYWARD**

Better this immersion than to live untouched

—LYNDA HULL

AUGUST MORNING, UPPER BROADWAY

As the body of the beloved is a window
through which we behold the blackness and vastness of space
pulsing with stars, and as the man

on the corner with his fruit stand is a window,
and the cherries, blackberries, raspberries
avocados and carrots are a rose window

like the one in Chartres, yes, or the one in Paris
through which light floods from the other world, the pure one
stabbing tourists with malicious abundant joy

though the man is tired in the summer heat
and reads his newspaper listlessly, without passion
and people pass his stand buying nothing

let us call this scene a window looking out
not at a paradise but as a paradise
might be, if we had eyes to see

the women in their swaying dresses, the season's fruit
the babies in their strollers infinitely soft: clear window
after clear window

THE LIGHT

What is the birthplace of the light that stabs me with joy
and what is the difference between avocados sold on the street
by a young man conceived in Delhi and avocados sold

in the West Side Market by cornrow girls, I am anyhow afloat
in tides of Puerto Rican, Cuban, Mexican, West Indian Spanish, wavelets of Urdu
swelling like oceans, sweating like jackhammers, rasping like crows, calling out

in the West Side Market, the Rite Aid, and every other shop on the street
Porque no comprendes, you don't own this city any more
the city belongs and has always belonged to its shoals of exiles

crashing ashore in foaming salty droplets, *como no, gringita*—
with their dances and their grandmothers, with their drinking and their violence
and their burning thirst for dignity, and smelling money, what, what is the joy

is it those lamps of light those babies in their strollers
those avocados with their dark-green pebbled rinds, shining from inside
two for four dollars in the West Side Market, and three for four dollars from the cart

joy like white light between the dollar bills, is it these volleys of light fired
by ancestors who remember tenements, the sweatshops, the war,
who supposed their children's children would be rich and free?

HOW FORTUNATE THE BOY

How fortunate the boy
    holding his father's hand
        crossing the street

coming home from a movie
    they let him stay
        up late to see

in the night and the rain
    the taxi making a left
        pulling him under its wheels

injuring the father
    instantly almost painlessly
        killing the boy so that he will never

suffer the disappointment
    of being a man
        lucky boy

child of our neighborhood vigil
    mourned by candlelight
        and news cameras

hero of our petition to the mayor
    about this bad intersection
        but the father is unfortunate

whose screams my neighbor says
    curdled her blood
        and the taxidriver is unfortunate

a man who will go on living
    making his living
        driving

MANAHATTA

I was asking for something specific and perfect for my city,
says Walt, lover of crowds, praiser of trades and occupations, celebrant
of the daily tide of immigrants, and I too seek the perfect image of you—

you mothering harbor, you royal sewer, you finger inside the sky
you dangling dream deferred, you queer hideout, you incubator of Jewish jazz,
you who exist as a landing field for helicopters, you whose laughter is heartless,

you digest dudes who crave to be bigshots, celebrities, hedge fund managers,
who like to show off and be bad, who get a kick
from cocaine. I am looking for a toaster in the hardware store, and here

two women stand behind a counter minding their cash registers
in their red apron uniforms. A points to B and says *You know
what she did Saturday? She went skinny-dipping.*

I have to wonder where. B looks pleased with herself. *The Harlem River.* Really?
it's where showoff boys used to dive and we giggling girls used to just watch
those bad boys. Times do change. B says, *I have to let my bad girl out sometimes.*

THE FIRST SNOWFALL

The first snowfall begins to turn grey.
A homeless guy lies across the freezing
sidewalk, hands shaking while the young cop gently asks

if he's sick. He says he is, and the cop asks
does he want to go to the hospital.
The guy's whole body has the shakes, a freezing night

is falling, they are waiting for an ambulance
and the men working at a parking garage down the block
lean on a Toyota, curious, watching, respectful.

Poor naked wretches, cries Shakespeare's Lear
in the voice of a man insane with grief
and indignation. Having grown up in the city,

I always thought it was poor *homeless* wretches.
Imagine rags as well as homelessness
on Shakespeare's streets as the snow pelted down

and began to turn grey, like here,
but with the filth of horses, no streetlights,
probably the watchman kicking you in the balls.

Nobody believes in the kindness of New Yorkers,
but I saw the drunk stretched boldly across the width
of sidewalk, the policeman being gentle to him,

the ER squad hoisting him into the van
being gentle, the men down the street
not laughing. Snow turning ashen. Nobody laughing.

THE GLORY OF CITIES

Let us now praise famous cities, our human fists against heaven, let us praise
    their devotion to wealth and power and art, goals toward which we swim
    ferociously upstream, tearing ourselves apart, to lay our eggs and die

along with swarms of our brothers and sisters, let me especially praise
    the cities of the Northeast Corridor from Boston to the District
    of Columbia, birth-lips of trade and industry, thumbs of unbeatable deals,

their mayors and their mistresses, their Chinese and Korean neighborhoods
    their Pakistani taxis, their Afro-American subway systems igniting
    their steel drum arpeggios, moonwalks, laden shopping bags, all superb

for staring at people while sinking into invisibility. Oh divine
    hot women, cool men, high school anarchists, weary waitresses and nurses
    hardhats off-shift, I follow underground boots to street, I watch this boy,

he is *off the boat,* he is thinking *food and freedom,* he is sending
    the money-order back home, it is so easy, there is a bank
    on every corner of the Upper West Side,

he is a little high, so when the officer detains him,
    he is slow producing his I.D. *Fuck. Fuck.*
    Watch his hands. Now watch the cop's fast hands.

BANGLADESH: THE DRIVER

It is where the driver was born
and still has family,
eighteen people to support.
I have thanked him for the Bollywood music
on his radio, and he sighs, a long elegiac sigh,
like a man who secretly knows how soon
the world will be under water
but does not wish to discuss it.

Everything is in the hands of the Gods.
Nonetheless he wishes to speak,
to explain his life to me, to say
In fifteen years he has had only one accident,
which was not at all his fault, the other guy
in the Lincoln actually ran the light,
but the police always think the taxi driver
is the guilty one.
It cost him four thousand dollars.
Now he is more cautious about everything,
like a turtle, he says, turning his head sharply.

In Bangladesh they drive even worse.
The death rate is terrible, but what are you
going to do? He gets out to open my door,
a courtesy unasked. His bald dome shines like brass
in the June sunset that tenderly strokes it
reaching across the Hudson
its cashless compensation.
He then undertakes a complicated mix
of bowing, smiling, and sighing, all at once,
but he is awkward. When I mirror his motion,
while handing over the two tens and three singles,
I too am awkward.

CINCO DE MAYO

What's that mob in the playground where I meant to sit
in sunshine read my book what's that uproar
P.S. 371 annual party a line for food
a dozen miniature soccer games around the pool no rules
backpacks of every hue parked on benches does nobody fear
theirs will be stolen? Are we really in the city or am I dreaming
three pretty *mariachis* singing *Cielito Lindo* and making
the children and their *mamacitas,* brown and beige,
sing along, everybody knows the words, indeed it is
New York City Upper West Side *Cinco de Mayo, querida*
they teach the children to dance *La cucaracha,* kick and shake
and shriek, for they say it is Mexican Independence Day
let the city employee hugging clipboard shake her hair loose
and if two days ago I was shopping for ant traps
and if three days ago I was fighting rush hour traffic, let there be
traffic traffic in another world for here it is spring
if we are ants crazy ants as I sometimes think
see we are musical ants we are dancing ants

BIKING TO THE GEORGE WASHINGTON BRIDGE

It sweeps away depression and today
you can't tell the heaped pin-white
cherry blossoms abloom along
Riverside Drive from the clouds above
it is all kerfuffle, all moisture and light and so
into the wind I go
past Riverside Church and the Fairway
Market, past the water treatment plant
and in the dusky triangle below
a hulk of rusted railroad bed
a single hooded boy is shooting hoops

It's ten minutes from here to the giant bridge
men's engineering astride the sky heroic
an animal roar of motors on it
the little red lighthouse at its foot
big brother befriending little brother
in the famous children's story
eight minutes back with the wind behind me
passing the boy there alone shooting
his hoops in the gloom

A neighborhood committee
must have said that space
should be used for something recreational
a mayor's aide must have said okay
so they put up basketball and handball courts
and if it were a painting or a photo
you would call it American loneliness

GHAZAL: THE MINIMUM WAGE, 2014

Having dinner before the president's state of the union address
my husband produces a rant on the topic of raising the minimum wage

He fumes as he has fumed on more than one occasion
it would be fucking good for the economy, raising the minimum wage.

He does not commonly use this language. We are microwaving the wild rice.
What would reduce income disparity, aid consumption? He shouts: a higher wage.

We are finishing the Thai spicy beef dish our granddaughter made
when she stayed over with us last weekend, cooking for no wage

but our love. We are eating spinach cooked with onions, coriander,
cardamom and butter. We agree that raising the minimum wage

has been shown by studies *not* to increase unemployment.
We fiercely interrupt each other to announce this, which is the wage

of marriage. Would congress approve a bill requiring companies like Walmart
and Target that employ more than x thousand people at minimum wage

to keep y percent as fulltime employees getting health benefits
along with their minimum starvation wage?

Not a chance, says my husband, not this broken congress, we pour another
glass of Argentinian Malbec, we drop the topic of the minimum wage,

I have a cookie with walnuts in it, the kind my granddaughter adores.
Soon we will see what the president says about the minimum wage.

A WALKER IN THE CITY II

> Crowds stagger sleeplessly through the boroughs
> As if they had just escaped a shipwreck of blood.

—FEDERICO GARCÍA LORCA, "A POET IN NEW YORK"

I could walk Broadway like bitter William Blake
wandering up and down Cheapside, like furious Lorca in Harlem
like LeRoi Jones at Columbia a Jonah angry enough to die

another poet disconsolate scowling enraged at body politic
lamenting the rich and the poor we always have with us
rich and poor whores, rich and poor slaves

the concrete marble and steel architecture glazed by human tears
the subway tunnel thick with rats
the halls of power also

numberless black men beaten strangled shot,
castrated odor of banks, briny fragrance of cash
demon sashaying with demon, garbage made visible

then sky over the river tangerine
a warm evening the Nigerian trumpeter on the corner
in his yellow and red superman t-shirt, on his folding chair,

no boombox, is cheerfully playing standards, here's How High
the Moon, not heard fifty years, a cute Jewish blue-eyed
brunette-with-stroller stops to let her baby listen,

the curly haired baby is into this music, his mouth open and drooling
his eyes wide, the woman and the musician chat—
the disconsolate walker is somewhat appeased by that.

WAITING FOR THE LIGHT

for Frank O'Hara

Frank, we have become an urban species
    at this moment many millions of humans are
        standing on some corner waiting like me

for a signal permitting us to go,
    a signal depicting a small pale pedestrian
        to be followed by a sea-green light

we do not use this opportunity
    to tune in to eternity
        we bounce upon our toes impatiently

It is a Thursday morning, Frank, and I feel
    rather acutely alive but I need a thing of beauty
        or a theory of beauty to reconcile me

to the lumps of garbage I cannot love enclosed
    in these tough shiny black plastic bags
        heaped along the curb of 97th Street, my street—

like a hideous reminder of the fate we all expect
    letting the bulky slimy truth of waste
        attack our esthetic sense and *joie de vivre*

reliably every Thursday. Let me scan the handsome amber
    columned and corniced dwellings
        reflected in rear windows of parked cars, let me wish

luck to their hives of intimacies, people
    in kitchens finishing a morning coffee
        saying *see you later* to the ones they live with

Let me raise my eyes to the blue veil adrift
    between and above the artifice of buildings
        and at last I am slipping through a flaw in time

where the string of white headlights approaching, the string
        of red taillights departing, seem as if
                they carry some kind of message

perhaps the message is that one block west
        Riverside Park extends its length
                at the edge of Manhattan like the downy arm

of a tender, amusing, beautiful lover,
        and after that is the deathless river
                but waiting for the light feels like forever

GHAZAL: AMERICA

My grandfather's pipe tobacco fragrance, moss-green cardigan, his Yiddish lullaby
when I woke crying: three of my earliest memories in America

Arriving on time for the first big war, remaining for the second, sad grandpa
who walked across Europe to get to America

When the babies starved, when the village burned, when you were flogged
log out, ship out, there was a dream, the green breast of America

My grandfather said no President including Roosevelt would save the Jews in Europe
he drew out an ample handkerchief and wiped away the weeping of America

One thing that makes me happy about my country
is that Allen Ginsberg could fearlessly write the comic poem "America"

Route sixty-six entices me westward toward dreaming California
I adore superhighways but money is the route of all evil in America

Let miners curse mines let workers curse bosses let football curse management
Let me curse the makers of bombs over Baghdad here in America

When I video your rivers your painterly meadows your public sculpture Rockies,
when I walk in your crooked cities I love you so much I bless you so much America

People people look there: grandpa please look: Liberty the Shekhina herself
welcoming you like a queen, like a goddess, to America

Take the fluteplayer from his mesa, take the raven from his tree
now that the buffalo is gone from America

White man, the blacks are snarling, the yellows swarming, the umber terrorists
are tunneling through and breathing your air of fear in America

If you will it, it is no dream, somebody admonished my grandfather
he surmised they meant survival in America

AFGHANISTAN: THE RAPED GIRL

Because the mullah raped her, she cannot be allowed to live
her brothers will kill her, it is a question of honor
she is ten years of age and does not yet menstruate
but bleeds like a stream in the hospital

The doctor finds the girl's mother holding her hand
both weeping, the mother saying
my daughter, may dust and soil protect you now
we will make you a bed of dust and soil
we will send you to the cemetery where you will be safe

The brothers have spoken to the police who command
the women's shelter where she now is staying
to release her to them
they have promised not to harm her
but everyone understands
lying is not a sin when one's honor is at stake

Even the mother understands this
even the child understands
only Dr. Sarwari, director of the shelter, is furious
she shouts at the police like a grey old crow
and the journalist who is doing his job
getting the story
may climb inside the bottle tonight

And I who read the story
will summon my mother, wherever she is
in the next world, perhaps in the paradise
she didn't believe
existed, she for whom honor
was not a concept, she from whom I learned
liberty and fury, our weapons in this world

> *New York Times, July 19, 2014. The italicized lines are from*
> *the New York Times story published in Heart online, October 2014*

Q&A: INSURANCE

If time is an arrow, what is its target

If a Flexible Flyer is the sled I had as a child, when may I become a child again

Do you need help digging the potatoes out of your garden of insults

Do you plan to vote in the next election

Is our country headed in the right direction or the wrong direction
     and what did the bulldozer tell the yellow helmet's ear

Which part of your body is like biting into a ripe peach
     which part shames you like a rotten banana

Would you like to find out how to lower your interest rate

When you go to heaven how old will you choose to be
     will you have cocktails on the well-watered lawn
          where Bach conducts Bach

Will you still chase after the Grateful Dead

Is your life like air leaking out of a balloon, or like rain falling on a pond
     dot dot dot   dear pocks   pocking the surface   dot dot dot
Can it be like snow falling on the ocean

Can desire drown you   like syrup over pancakes

When an ambulance siren wakes you at 3 a.m. do you feel relieved
     not to be strapped to that stretcher
          speeding toward the grim unknown
               do you then snuggle next to someone

Are you satisfied with your detergent

Can you name a more perfect irony than the new world trade center, sacred icon
     of capitalism, revered lingam of profit, soaring above the memorial pools
          of people killed when the first towers fell

Can you describe the scent of dried blood

What about the smell of iron chains in your cell
    can you sing the threnody of the maggots

When I removed my mask did I frighten you
    like a drone crossing your sky

Are you satisfied with your auto insurance

When ecstasy approaches why do you resist
    What are you afraid of
        Can you please unbutton your shirt now

MAKING A MEAL OF THEM

for Dunya Mikhail

The air remains full of sunlight

—JEAN FOLLAIN, "THE ART OF WAR"

Because we love what makes us feel alive
what makes us feel something instead of nothing

be it a dimpled infant or a snowy January sunrise
be it a mine disaster or a flood or a roadkill deer

today I will make a meal of several wars we enjoy
watch me swallow down the six million plus

gypsies homosexuals the feeble plus
the sixty million and more

mentioned by Morrison in the dedication
to *Beloved* for there are things we eat to live

and things we eat for entertainment
for the tang of poison, the sugar of cruelty, like

cupcake icing the tongue appreciates plus why not
while we are here together Vilna Dresden

Nanjing Nagasaki Palestine Baghdad the Congo
The former Yugoslavia plus

the other Americas, United Fruit smiling
La Virgen weeping *Los Indios* bleeding

(It is more than a meal, it is a banquet
it is almost staggering)

And here I am sucking that blood
in the land of the free

in the land of the free and the drugged
in the country of credit

all of us vampires and voters, all of us sports fans
all of us readers and writers of righteous tweets

all of us shoppers all of us holy innocents
sucking it up brushing our capital teeth

DARE I CALL YOU COUSIN

for Afaa Weaver, and for Frances Payne Adler, who made the video

A wall is a symbol of safety that never works,
it didn't keep the Mongols out,
it tightens the fear inside you like a buckle.

We reach the Ramallah checkpoint at 5.a.m.
The video camera scans a large barred cage,
The crowd inside is a mass of noisy animals.

A child is crying, Papa, I have to pee.
The camera turns to a dark-eyed Israeli soldier
perhaps first time in life away from mama

who stands unmoving, doesn't look, doesn't listen
taught to transform the mirror of his soul,
those fathomless brown eyes, into a wall.

We know that fear is crushing
souls on both sides of the wall
and from these grapes we know what wine will flow.

TEMBLOR

The earth snapped . . .

—KATHRYN SCHULZ, *THE NEW YORKER*

At the edge of the world California has all one needs, unlimited sea and sand
mountains and sky above, canyons, vineyards, and the fault zone—

moonrise over dunes, long shadows, dry heat departing,
and in her room a woman leans toward a screen

learning about some beheadings performed by men
who have surrendered to a god with a sword

because surrender to a god is like the swoon of a girl
the pain of living becomes so sweet and if there is a sword all the better

get your hands on an uzi you will show those infidels what faith is
the woman is trying to understand their frenzy

a crack in earth a crust then a body
dragged beneath it

    *

Decades since the bus from Boston to Alabama, a summer of love
of justice, discipline and fear, the toilet smell of the sheriff's breath

scent of magnolia and honeybaby sweat, kids chanting *Hell no, we won't go*
peace signs like an encoded seraphic message everyone got, and now

only the impulse to hurl things at the screen when the talking heads come on
saying *nuke 'em,* they spread their thick owl wings, they twitch

their coyote noses, she is a rabbit in the harsh grass paralyzed
and she knows that in less than three seconds there will be a commercial

for cars, then one for a cosmetic product, then one for a congressman
while the wars cough up phlegm of amnesia

crack in her mind
unrelenting pressure beneath it

*

To the naked eye the motions of earth are imperceptible
the plates sliding north at the rate her fingernails grow

from the air no hint of violence, rather a long wrinkled scar, looking old
and harmless, like herself, but where the fault curves the grinding proceeds

she wonders why she imagines killing the killers
when her deep heart's core wants peace and linnet's wings not owls'

yet she sometimes pictures driving her car into a wall, or into a crowd
and she likes the fun of throwing glass things, wine bottles, into the yellow

recycle pail to hear them crash, she likes tugging weeds up by muddy roots
dear aged lady whose garbage will be "picked up" for a monthly fee

sorted and
buried or burnt far away

*

Against havoc, to join committees, to march, to sing, slowly to come
to understand, to write, to raise your voice against the compulsive lie,

do these slight geological tremors satisfy your craving to change
the laws of history, to speak the unspoken, do they pacify

your stifled impulse to murder the secretary of defense
the moon still rises with the serenity of a duchess

The coyotes still trot through the sagebrush in that eerie light
their eyes penetrate shadows, they lift their voices in an ancient song

the wind blows wherever it wants to, the television confidently sneers
the sea is never full, back and forth it daily slides, sandpipers dancing at its edge

and your poetry also makes nothing happen except among the synapses
that are whispering *only connect* to each other

and the desperate force inside each
crying *break*

THE LIBERAL ARTS

In mathematics they say the most beautiful solution is the correct one
In physics they say everything that *can* happen *must* happen
In history they say the more it changes the more it is the same

In astrophysics you take the long view
In chemistry you explode and blend, it is a bit like freestyle cooking, the Yiddish
     term would be: you potschke
In biology you smell the flowers, the enticing flowers, and you play with mice, and
     you write grant proposals

In jurisprudence they say there is no justice
In philosophy they say there is no truth
In literary studies they say everybody come along be ironic now

Business school we systematize the competitive strategies we learned in the sandbox
Engineering moves us firmly into manhood, we grip the material world in our fists
Computer science assists us toward the goal of replacing our species with a new,
     improved, more efficient form of life, based in electronics instead of carbon—
     many of us
     are rushing to transform ourselves as quickly as possible

Religion is still hot
People keep plunging passionately into and out of it at the usual brisk rate
Geography suggests the future dominance of North America by Spanish
     speaking people
     but it does not say when; geology looks stony, takes the long view

Music bridges mathematics, the soul of the universe, and my personal soul
Visual art is the bridge between my bag of body and bones and stuff in the painterly
     universe
Drama crosses this bridge on foot

In the novel they say omit nothing, harvest the entire goddamn world
In memoir they say the self is silently weeping, give it a tissue
In poetry they say the arrow may be blown off course by storm and returned by
     miracle

TO CHARLIE, ON HIS POETRY

for C. K. Williams, 1936–2015

Confession implies shame
you had none of that

you did those c-scans
of your own mind shamelessly,

following every fold, penetrating
every layer: the mind looking at itself,

the mind examining itself—Guilt yes,
bitter anger yes, obstinate lust yes,

like a carnival ride, the gilded car
careening all over the area, zipping, bumping,

to a viewer it might seem out of control
but no, it was only passionately honest.

The zoom of your poem would often
pull far out from the scene you were capturing,

then you would nail it, down to the last
pixel of the truth.

The truth was not inscrutable
but it resisted, it wanted to wrestle.

Fear yes, doubt absolutely, and don't forget
sweet love, breaching like a dolphin

above its salty element in the little
book of tender funny love poems

to Catherine who is a real
person in them, no puppet.

A glad splashing in that book
a sinking afterward

the body in terror turning to words
remembering perhaps the physicist

John Wheeler in a lecture explaining
that the universe exists in order to be

perceived, observed, *seen* by consciousness
that it's a kind of evolving uroboros

your task was to do some of that seeing—
as much as time would allow—

no matter how crazy it seemed. I will miss
those gritty poems in your sandy voice.

I mention all this to you
who didn't believe in an afterlife

because you may have been mistaken
about that, and wherever you are

whatever form you occupy next
should remember how strong

and accurate your seeing was,
and be a little bit happy about it.

UNDERGROUND

Meandering through libraries as I like to do, among books, those doomed   artifacts,
I run across by accident or by virtue of good karma in a previous life

a book of photographs of the underground railroad done cleverly
movingly as collages incorporating nineteenth century contexts and today's as well
the rivers the woods

the barns the farmhouses the churches the mansions, the trapdoors the tunnels the attics
the classified advertisements seeking to sell slaves in lots of four or forty or more

offering rewards for the escaped ones — no ideology but business
the farmer who faced down the sheriff regarding the slaves he was hiding

by pointing to the upstairs windows at which his four sons stood holding rifles
the freed blacks of the north with their white colleagues

John Brown's grave a photo of Tubman a white scarf at her neck the Quaker Levi
    Coffin
the handsome Frederick Douglas the handsome underground stationmaster William Still

saving and saving
the opposite of wounding and wounding.

The book claims the underground railway was integrated and was the first example of
    true integration in American history. It is a black man claiming this, oh
I cannot say how cheered I am at any moment to be reminded human decency
and courage exist like fierce white blood cells in our organism

for it is difficult to find words of hope regarding decency and courage
while words of the unhealed wound are everywhere

while bodies continue bleeding, officials continue denying, op-eds continue decrying
because the language of hope is underground

GHAZAL: AMERICA THE BEAUTIFUL

Do you remember our earnestness our sincerity
in first grade when we learned to sing America

The Beautiful along with the Star-Spangled Banner
and say the Pledge of Allegiance to America

We put our hands over our first grade hearts
we felt proud to be citizens of America

I said One Nation Invisible until corrected
maybe I was right about America

School days school days dear old Golden Rule Days
when we learned how to behave in America

What to wear, how to smoke, how to despise our parents
who didn't understand us or America

Only later learning the *Banner* and the *Beautiful*
live on opposite sides of the street in America

Only later discovering the Nation is divisible
by money by power by color by gender by sex America

We comprehend it now this land is two lands
one triumphant bully one still hopeful America

Imagining amber waves of grain blowing in the wind
purple mountains and no homeless in America

Sometimes I still put my hand tenderly on my heart
somehow or other still carried away by America

Q & A: REALITY

Did Max Planck really say "I regard matter as derivative from consciousness"

Did Sir James Jeans, pioneering physicist, really say "the universe begins to look
    more like a great thought than a great machine"

Was that you I saw smiling with perfect teeth in the ad for spring travel wear,
seated on the hull of a sailboat with a companion whose teeth surpassed perfection,
he leaning on right elbow and you with left hand resting on that glossy hull, its man-
    go-tinted lacquer the item that really catches one's eye, shining and hard

Was your parka in the ad really that yellow or was it enhanced by Photoshop

When we have finished describing the elephant, will we have an elephant

Would you be willing to participate in a survey

Can you make galactic mid-air swirls like kids on skateboards

Do you understand that your consent to things as they are has been manufactured
by history and film, and that there is no blue guitar because all guitars, even those
    made hard and shining by layers of lacquer, are cherry-brown, and they fuck you
    up, your mom and dad

Does this enrage you

Do you think it is a matter of indifference, in other words do you consent

Did you once wonder how a huge contraption of metal could ever take flight

Did you once mistake causality for casualty

Why do you guess the admen included an American flag in the picture of the
shiny yacht's hull, along with you in the yellow parka, your companion in subdued
    nautical rainwear, both of you with strangely white teeth

Do you remember the name of the congressman who said, "if it's a legitimate rape,
    the female body has ways to shut that whole thing down," meaning that a raped
    woman will not conceive a child, and so there is no need for abortion, and did he
    really say that at a prayer breakfast

Do you agree that the arc of the moral universe is long, but it bends toward justice

Why would you think that

Was Nicola Tesla influenced by Vedic philosophy

Is it true that what the imagination seizes as beauty must be truth whether it existed before or not

Is it true that looking for consciousness in the brain is like looking in the radio for the announcer

Is it true that when election results are accepted by the populace and the media, that means the election was honest (or we do not care if it was honest or not)

Do you remember what you wrote in my high school yearbook

If we dove into a cosmic wormhole could we choose to emerge in the Eisenhower years when the world was all before us, expanding, and we too were expanding, like light! right there along with it, ballgame after ballgame, and we were indisputably the good ones

Did the Stone Age end because of a lack of stones

Approaching Eighty: New Poems (2010–2019)

*

The well of the deep wants us
The deep life—sex, god, death—it *wants* us

—KAZIM ALI

WHAT THE BUTTERFLY IS THINKING

Not anxiety-prone like me, it is not thinking about extending its brief life
or the serenade of iridescent blue patches on its taffeta wings

or the war. Or any of the other wars. Or the moon afloat on winter water.
I am putting money on this. I lick it like ice. I am confident.

The motions of many creatures appear random
but are not? My husband says cows and bees—

cows and bees are swimming in his mouth
cows browsing around in two sluttish dimensions, bees in three or four

among the savage perfumes, scavenging for the tastiest weeds strewn here and there
he says. The biggest nourishment bang for a bite, or sweet for a single suck

is why they never ever
form straight lines.

Really? In the lavender bush fifty seething bees, a dressy graduating class, lifting
hovering descending & travelling to another flower entirely. Girls just want

to have fun. Orderly? Purposeful? Please come
back, every iridescent blue-winged thing.

Come land
on my hand.

NOVEMBER ELEVENTH: TWO POEMS

Walt, do you mind if I climb on your shoulders

I remember the time I sat on my father's shoulders
wearing my itchy blue sailor dress with the white stripes
to watch an Armistice Day parade

surrounded by people enjoying thoughts of peace
I too gladdened by thoughts of peace up there on my father's shoulders
where I could see above the heads

of the crowd, could feel proud (mother explained) Armistice Day
was my birthday; today the day is re-named Veterans Day, to celebrate
the fact of war, as if we needed

yet another holiday celebrating war, none celebrating peace—
but forget that. Looking over the heads of the crowd watching the marchers
march in their uniforms, the brass band play

their banging exuberant music; girls high-stepping and tossing batons
oh how enjoyable peace was
on my father's shoulders

childhood memories are like ghosts
not all ghosts want to strangle you
sometimes they come to bless

I am attempting

I am attempting to see
over the heads of the crowd
I know she is there marching

I like how the confetti
blowing past her is tinted
every pastel shade, I like...

Goddess,

turn your face to me

then I'll see you

I like being taller than my father . . .

APPROACHING EIGHTY, BIKING UP PROSPECT

One of those blithe summer afternoons that used to last forever
biking up Prospect Street for dinner and a movie

trees along the street like affectionate cousins
willing to discuss family secrets

I say: the air is so tender it seduces you into believing
that a kelson of the creation is love

he says: we've evolved to feel good at moderate temperatures
such as this and uncomfortable when it is hotter or colder

I say: it appears we are actually coexistent with the universe
like salt in water and smoke in atmosphere

he says: maybe so
being a scientist he hedges his bets

being a scientist he pursues the reality beneath the surface
being a poet so do I

when we brake our bikes at a light I quietly look at him
the light changes and we cross

THE TRANSITION: FIVE POEMS

Letters

You whom I loved
whose letters I kept
you all know who you are

now know that I could not save you
I am doing the age-appropriate thing
returning to my roots

in a New York City apartment
yet my fingers have touched every letter
and postcard in these boxes and envelopes

I have read many
I have kissed many goodbye
pressing my lips to paper

some have made me laugh or cry
I will keep some small fraction
to read again

what is the use of apologies
there is never enough love
but I did

love you
and now the attic
is bare boards and a hanging bulb

Selling the house

The attic is empty now
bare boards and a hanging bulb

the basement is sealed against flooding
like a veteran who can't remember a thing

painters have plastered over the crater
where my son punched a wall

my study offered me language and happiness
I hereby abandon it but I hope the buyer

will soon enjoy a cascade of creativity
and may she and her husband contribute

pleasurable odors to the master bedroom
may their girls post pop-star images above their beds

let the living room fill itself with music
the dining room with conversation

let the kitchen
never lack for garlic and wine

may cardinals and jays continue flashing
their color wheels outside the kitchen window

let the laundry alcove my husband created
pride itself on its convenience

let the big back yard
be flowery and herbal

Oh house, please don't cry
I mean these words for a blessing to you

Paint Fumes

They have been painting our house all week
to get it pretty so we can sell it

the whole process is disorienting
am I making a terrible mistake

all these years wanting to live in the city
wanting to leave the pale suburb

is my brain a mere cauliflower
now I am lying in bed trying to nap

breathing the fumes shallowly
as if they are less poisonous that way

as if I can sleep and be a new person
when I wake up

here in my humbling dotage
of what delusion am I not capable

Selection

The selection of books takes months
I feel exactly like a Nazi officer
sending some to the left some to the right

deciding which happy few I might read again, feeling the tension
gripping their pages like teens at a dance, players before a game—
finding homes for the wallflowers, the benched ones

in libraries flea markets second-hand bookstores
sadly I throw away the ragged ones, the ones
I have abused by excessive attention, I release them

from their suffering—goodbye dear college anthologies
I learned names and dates from your pages
I learned the passions exaltation and despair

Piano

Any takers for this poor old piano
top of the line three quarters
of a century ago
in need of cleaning
in need of tuning
myself in need of getting rid of it
right now
and the music trapped in its body

THEY ARE ALWAYS ASKING

They are always asking
What it is like
to be so

ancient so superannuated
it means they want to know
my thoughts about death

in some ways my relation
to death is
that of a daughter

to her mother
loving and angry
distant and needy

or that of a woman
rejecting the brutish lies
of patriarchy

while at the same time
embracing some
particular man

or like a hippie beating
her breast still crazy
after all these years

hiking the desert
torch in hand
in broad daylight

THIRST

for Marilyn Krysl

It is not that the old are wise
but that we thirst for the wisdom

we had at twenty
when we understood everything

when our brains bubbled
with tingling insights

percolating up from
our brilliant genitals

when our insurgent music struck
like a sudden August hurricane

thundering along the Florida coast
battering down the world's hypocrisies

oh then we knew the truth
then we sparkled like mica in granite

and now we stand on the shore
of an ocean that rises and rises

and is too salt to drink

APPROACHING EIGHTY: SIX POEMS

The distraction

A wide screen a wild scream, a rosy dream, a white screen

    —they have left the theater like a flock of birds—

    of which she retains neither images nor words

Or: she is sometimes inattentive
she means to put the forks and knives away
    back in the drawer

In her peeling yellow kitchen
which is like a
    warm old shawl to her

and begins by walking in exactly the wrong direction
or her arm reaches for the wrong drawer
    before she catches it

laughs at herself for being wrong again

    —laughter the overcoat of her fear—

    caw caw the interior crow

Plastic

Every time she throws away some stupid plastic object
some microwave safe container of blueberries
some set of plastic plates for appetizers
to feed visitors whom she does not love
she grieves a little in her heart
she mourns a little
she despises her unalleviated wastefulness
she regrets her late capitalist consumerism
she feels like a watermelon of pollutant
greasy ash in the kidneys of earth
she feels she is murdering her mother
why did she let this plastic into her life

When the fog rises

Obliterating
what lies in front of her
so that she must concentrate in order not to trip

when the crabby shell of ego hardens
when she becomes impenetrable
when nothing can cause her to fear, rejoice, or hope

she explains to her friend
my brain cells are settling down to being mulch—
her friend admonishes her not to think that way

but to say to herself
those old brain cells have had their chance
they're tired, it's time for them

to step away from the table
give some new brain cells a chance
to show what they can do

an attempt at humor
to which she replies
peering through the fog:
as if . . .

*

words gone
back where they came from

The years

Between when she held a man's penis
like a flag
for the first time

and the final
time not quite yet
arrived

the years
the years
ah the years

Ballad

after Leonard Cohen

Some lights are moving toward me
some lights are leaving fast
it isn't that I ever thought
my little life would last

I'm cooking in my kitchen
I'm climbing into bed
I'm pushing eighty but my sweet
I still am giving head

Some lights are growing brighter
some lights are going out
black lives always in danger
white lives eaten by doubt

The sky is turning apple red
and then it falls to gloom
the world's most lofty towers
stood up like dicks—then boom
    stood up, and then boom boom

Some lights call me to party down
some lights have blown a fuse
ten illnesses wait patiently
one life is mine to lose

Yours is the joke that makes me laugh
the frown that makes me cry
so many years together, love
don't leave me high and dry

Some lights are moving toward me
some lights are leaving fast
it isn't that I ever thought
my little life would last

Blizzard

When it begins to snow hard
in the violet night outside

she wants to swing open a door
face the murderous wind out there prepared

never to see the sun enthroned again
in the gold and magenta settings Hollywood loves

never to see the moon race midnight's clouds
like the trailer for a fifties noir film

stepping across the lintel and pressing on
into the zooming flying tiny ice petals

pulling in her breath
she will finally know who she is

like a wild dog she will no longer
have to heel or sit, or stay or fetch

so many awakenings
only one small death

READING DAN BEACHY-QUICK, WONDERFUL INVESTIGATIONS

The lightning struck him and left a scar.
The wind stopped blowing and the wheat stood up.

— DAN BEACHY-QUICK, "LINES"

The relation of a poem to time is as follows:
a narrative poem travels along a stream
creating white ruffles
of water behind it
swimming over rocks it arrives at the ocean and dies

A lyric poem unlocks a door in the stream
taking one deep breath it walks through the door
into a big square lobby in the sky
where Time Present greets it
smiling her dazzling hostess smile

Time Present reassures the lyric poem:
you are back home now in eternity
nothing to fear so take it easy my dear
Time Past won't hurt you any more he can't get in
would you like to order something at the bar

Travelling the stream's white rapids
or glancing around eternity's buffed white clouds
like breasts in a sheer blue blouse
the poem speaks its mind
And as soon as a thing is said

it becomes true
if it is a poem

if it does not become true
it was not a poem

NAMING THE THIRST AGAIN

When we are born
thirst makes us cry

thirst surges through our arteries
when the hormones hit

when we start to wither
our thirst intensifies

for the tongue of touch
the magazine of rain

we remember we were once loved
love kept us alive

    ***

the mother's face
was the face of God

the berries in the bucket
were sweet to the taste

we were swifter than eagles
stronger than lions

when was this
it was in our dream

and when we wake
all gone but the thirst

    ***

now we pause to watch
sparrows compete in a puddle

now we peer into a stroller
at a months-old face

now we reach for something
to give the homeless man

we thirst for love in our dream
we are sparrows

and babies and beggars
we must drink our thirst

THE SEA

I see the sea, I see the sea, said the boy
is it white as an angel's beard, said the girl
no, it is black as a shovel in hell, said the boy

I'll dig to heaven with it, said the girl
what is heaven, said the boy
run home to your mother, said the girl

is she in the refrigerator, said the boy
no, she is in the three wire mousetraps, said the girl
I can hear them from the clouds, said the boy

then lend me your library, said the girl
the one with the sealskin umbrella, said the boy
the one with a chorus singing, said the girl

those mice and those birds
and my mother, said the boy

*

So then I began to ask the truculent boy
is my dear friend thinking about death

like somebody trying on a coat or a cape
or a pair of boots preparing for winter

or is he looking at maps
for his next adventure

is it a path out of the turgid swamp
where a moment ago there appeared no path

if the air he breathes reminds him it has traveled
through the hived lungs of the dead

will he cough alarmingly
like an Andean lion sniffing rabbit

and then shall I offer him my glass
emptied of loss

*

It is natural to think of the sea
when we think of birth and death said the girl
we screen a heaving sea video in our empurpled minds

what do you mean by screen, said the boy
is it something like scream
or is it more like drawing a veil, like hiding

from the truth
what is truth, said the girl glancing
at the sublime surges and heaves of the sea

and the lyric spill of the surf going on
harmonious like birth and death in her mind
and all that spins violently among the stars

like refugees under water said the boy
glancing shyly at the green idea of drowning

MY MOTHER REFUSED TO WEED

She had lived through
depression and war
she had been glad to leave the city
she wanted nothing to die
she wanted everything to flourish and thrive
when she planted she crumbled clods by hand
her garden was a thriving mess
some years a hall of sunflowers
a tornado of candy colored cosmos some years
"dependable beauty" said the catalog
we have photos of her
in a peasant blouse in that garden laughing
wearing her mortality on her face that was never veiled
the flowers shoulder high she was so small
ultimately raspberries took over
thorny canes arched across her cement walk
a sign of pride and a problem for the mailman but he forgave her
I wanted her to cut them but she refused
the berries were so delicious she explained
she wanted to feed me
and feed me

MOTHER IN THE ASSISTED LIVING

1. We are at a table by ourselves
she has accused the staff of stealing her bathing suit
and the other guests of being mean to her

2. She raises her chin
she says she sticks up for herself
we have had this conversation before

3. The staff is mostly Dominican
she says the staff is anti-Semitic
or they hate her because she is small

4. My husband does not visit because the smell
makes him ill
he says and I understand this

5. She shows me her room with the plant on the windowsill
she shows me where she stores
leftovers from her dinners

6. When I visit I trim her white naturally curly hair,
she has no idea that she is beautiful
as the shekhina herself

and I tweeze her facial hairs
because she does not want to look like the bearded
lady in the circus

then I hug her and she hugs me like a clamp
off we go for a ride
to the mall

time travels like the wind
and in the fall the maples along the turnpike
sway with mature pride

the pure pride of survival

OLD WOMAN AT THE RIVER

On the bank of the river
I slide inside my sleeping bag
sleep is good if I am not
kept awake by coughing
the sound of the water soothes
time passes and does not pass
when I am better I will sit
and meditate for a while
there may be birds to listen to
then I will step down the bank
and put my naked foot in the water
which will shock at first,
being so cold, so swift.

A SEASON OF ACID RAIN

We like to lay our heads on Gaia's breasts
Gaia's breasts pouring milk
the weeds growing out of her hands
the birds and insects flitting from her scalp
her grey bones challenging our climb
dragon fire from her mouth
but now her tears—we didn't know a goddess could cry
or that the tears of a goddess could be contaminated
mother please stop it
we do not like to see our mother cry

UTOPIAN

My neighbor's daughter has created a city
you cannot see
ruled by a noble princess and her athletic consort
all the buildings are glass so that lies are impossible
beneath the city they have buried certain words
which can never be spoken again
chiefly the word divorce which is eaten by maggots
when it rains you hear chimes
rabbits race through its suburbs
the name of the city is one you can almost pronounce

ROUFFIGNAC

Bear-claw scratches have engraved the walls
now we are a kilometer deep says the guide

the horses appear to smile the mammoths gravely
parade across the limestone vault above us

they have inhabited the ceiling along with dozens
of other animals for twenty thousand years

I cannot leave I feel my pulse
my breath slower and slower

In Cap Blanc the horses are dignified
In Lascaux they gallop

twenty thousand years ago we pressed
palms against stone we sprayed red

pigment over and around them
some of us were only children

some of us thought they themselves were horses
or bison and my husband says do you notice

we have seen thousands of animals painted and carved
none fighting—what does this tell us

about the people
about the artists

THE DEATH OF THE SWAN, AND OTHER QUESTIONS

After many a summer, does the swan die?
    Yes, after many a summer the swan does die.

Left alone, would people hate each other and make war?
    My mother said they would not.

—Lapel needs straightening. —Leave me alone, will you?
    —I will never leave you alone.

Yesterday seems so far away, doesn't it?
    Yes, and it will never return, not until time swallows her yellow tail.

Old man river, do you trust him to flow forever?
    I do, deeply.

Unlike the turnpike traffic on Friday night?
    The turnpike traffic cannot flow forever; ultimately it will rust.

Nothing really touches you does it?
    I don't have to answer that question.

Everything frightens you?
    If you say that again I'll punch you in the mouth.

Even your own son, running hopefully toward you?
    You have heard of the sins of the fathers.

Do you not wish you knew how to love me?
    I wish scrambled eggs and a side of bacon.

—Nevertheless I move. —Can you move on?
    —On and off, I can. I can and I will. Bye.

Is it true that we can only be hurt by those we love?
    No, it is not true. Not at all.

THE ROSE TREE

Phi Beta Kappa poem, Princeton University 2019

What is called fate or destiny
need not be predictable

only yesterday you were a giraffe
and today you are a zebra

a mathematician who falls asleep twisted in frustration
wakes with the solution blinking on his frontal lobe

he is happy as a child who has learned to unknot a shoelace
and a tax lawyer suddenly captured by an idea of justice

feels like a teenage surfer pulled by a speedboat
zipping through lake water, and decides to run for congress

while a high school girl biting her hair-ends thinks
Nothing is sweeter than wisdom, which makes her laugh

for she has read that brains run on glucose
and it's fun to think that reading is like candy

although she knows that narwhals and frogs are endangered
that oceans rise and icebergs melt and fire devours

and that the human animal is a mountain of greed
a creature of irrational cruelty

still, numberless men and women roll the rock
of truth uphill, solve problems, heal wounds

nobody knows where ideas come from
they come like love, impossible to anticipate

yesterday you were a greenish stalk
today you are a rose tree

THE LAPTOP ALSO IS DYING

Born in the last decade of the last,
I mean previous, century,

It took me awhile to recognize
that she was ready to die.

first she became unable to remember where
things were, then every gesture and motion slowed

and sometimes halted and had to be restarted
while a strange rainbow wheel endlessly whirled on the screen

like something ecstatic bursting out of Ezekiel
that might be wordless laughter or a yell

the long interval between my thought and her response
inevitably disturbed me. I understood

she meant this as a message
about life, about the world

in which everything winds down
and we cannot help grieving,

but what a couple, what a *pair* we were,
humming with energy back then we flew

intermingled and interchanged our ghosts
our ancestors like shadows while we flew

and *she* was also a *he* or no gender at all, like a cloud, like dust
back then, back then, when we needed to propose

a new song for the God we don't believe in
an argument for the God we wanted to love

THE WORDS WHEN I WROTE THEM

When she was two, and made to hike with the rest of us,
our younger daughter toddled on her fat little legs

across the soft beach singing "I don't know, I don't know,
I don't know, I don't know" to the tune of "Twinkle, twinkle,

little star," I still remember that, and she has spent
a lifetime learning what she does not know,

because she is a scientist, but all of us are seekers, in our way,
all of us still learning what to think of ourselves and the world.

When H. D. was an old lady like me,
a voice commanded her *Write, write or die.*

The words when I wrote them were oddly familiar
ocean-floor exoskeletal creatures, glossy, lumpy, waving tails

or waving tentacles. To me it was beautiful and good
down there, but I don't know. I only collected them,

hoisted them from deep to daylight, nearly drowning
and here I am gasping, pulling off my mask, breathing.

BIKING RIVERSIDE DRIVE AGAIN

Handsome old whitebeard
wearing camo and big boots
walking past won't smile

back when I smile at him
most men do but this one is stone
it makes me wonder what he saw
in the war

ELEANOR, 1884–1962: FIVE POEMS

When will our consciences grow so tender that we will act
to prevent human misery rather than avenge it?

—ELEANOR ROOSEVELT

1. The Mountain

Difficult to say what the supreme
moment is in the life of a mountain,
but in your sixties when they made you a delegate

to the United Nations you pushed through
a finished draft of the Universal Declaration of Human Rights.
You insisted the phrase all men are born free and equal

be changed to say all human beings,
you graciously forced the other delegates to compromise
with one another on wording. To get it done. And it was done.

2. The Streams

You had that form Helen Hokinson cartooned
in The New Yorker for decades, the stout pouter-pigeon
shape of the society lady,

you had your mother's neglect, your drunken father's
splashy promises, his death, your mother-in-law's rules,
you had Franklin's lifelong infidelity,

you had a brilliant Frenchwoman teacher and some friends who loved
your intelligence and goodness, you had at least
one woman lover,

everything somehow converging, like the streams to the Hudson River
over near Val-Kill, for the point of suffering
is to make one compassionate

to make one act on behalf of the defeated
to make one breathe the soiled breath of the poor
to make the demand that the rules change.

3. The Ribbon

While Woody Guthrie walked that ribbon of highway
looking at that endless skyway, and while John
Steinbeck followed the dust storms west,

you feared being the Governor's wife, the President's wife,
the irritating visits, the awful balls
where Franklin flirted with everyone

but when you discovered you could charm and organize,
could drive the Cadillac of politics throughout this mighty land
where banks were made of marble and people were growing hungrier,

your trilling feminine voice enunciated the duties of privilege:
opposition to lynching, support for a World Court
and for slum dwellers, miners, dirt farmers, negroes, Jews, women—

You bucktoothed horse-faced woman
at the golden end of the ladder of class—
a man like Guthrie and his guitar at the dustbowl end

twanging this land is your land, this land is my land,
the ribbon connecting you, you with the FBI file of 3000 pages
and a Klan bounty of twenty-five thousand on your head—

They called your husband "that man in the White House,"
they said Roosevelt was really Rosenberg,
they said you were Commie Jews,

they laughed at your ugliness,
they laughed at your quivering voice,
they laughed at you over cigars and whiskey,

(that is what pigs do, they laugh
with a nasty snorting sound
in their sty, that they take for the world)

4. The Brink, 1939

A war, and then the fantasy of peace like a canoe headed smoothly,
unstoppably toward Niagara, you think no, please, but there's the roar
ahead, the mist. Still, on the brink, My country 'tis of thee,

Sweet land of liberty sounds utterly real in Marion Anderson's big
black contralto, when you quit the whites-only Daughters
of the American Revolution that refuses to invite her

to sing in their hall, when instead you arrange the gig
on the Lincoln Memorial steps, and the crowd fills the Mall
with tears. As if we the people believed in justice for all.

5. Diana the Huntress in Camouflage

Before someone invented pills for depression, you wrote:
If anyone looks at me, I want to weep.
My mind goes round and round like a squirrel in a cage,
I want to run and I can't and I despise myself,

and proceeded to compose your syndicated column
"My Day" daily for twenty-two years, offering advice and opinions,
your prose domestic as a peony centerpiece
on a polished cherrywood table,

the way you might say to the man, Now, Franklin, you should—
or remark, when some weary delegates wished to quit for the day,
I drive hard, and when I get home I will be tired,
and so will the gentlemen on this committee,

in which fashion you obtained much of what you wanted
oh woman of pragmatic subtle strategy—
your quivering mind packed with the arrows of liberty
free and equal, the joy of the hunt, the lay of the land

under your feet as you ran together with your band of friends.

JANUARY 15, 1991: THE FIRST GULF WAR

I was leaving the synagogue after the seminar
my left breast was already down the river
the scar well on its way to healing
myself partially ready for the future,

the guard outside the exit door said bombs
were falling on Baghdad. I didn't recite a psalm.
Before I knew what I was saying or doing
I leaned on a lamppost, rested forehead on arm,

whispered, "I wish I didn't live to see this fucking slaughter."
When I repeated that on the phone to my daughter
she scolded me for saying it. Right. Only the thing
is, although that war was swift as water

spiraling down a drain, then came cascades
of wars streaming after, dominoes of invasions
that are clacking away still at their merciless killing—
not the blessing I planned for my latter days.

FROM **AFTER INAUGURATION**

Chapter One: Inauguration

As you have heard, a new king rose over Egypt
a rabid creature in the shape of a man
lacking a conscience
a man with small hands
a rubbery pink mouth
that poured lies like oil
emitted hatred like carbon dioxide
greedy to devour men, women and children
like hamburgers
of constant adulation
and the spirits of women everywhere rose up
and on a determined day they marched
in the capital city and many other cities
they marched for kindness
and dignity in this world
they filled the streets and highways
with love and song
they took photographs of each other's witty signs
they mocked the king
they marched with babies and men of good heart
they rallied
they returned to their homes
but the king was still there—the king still sat
on his throne of money
End of chapter one

Chapter Two: Executive Order

A stroke of the pen
what good what harm
a stroke of the pen
like a twist of the arm

a stroke of the pen
like a puppy's turd
a stroke of the pen
certain acts of murder

A stroke of the pen
in the war against women
the smirks of the men
are always well-hidden

Except for the man
most powerful on the earth
finger above the button
how gaily he smirks

A stroke of the pen—
a keyboard tap
in the devil's den
a devil's crap.

Chapter Three: The Funhouse

Speeding through the funhouse   tunnel, catching glimpses of
myself in the funhouse   mirrors, unlike the mirrors
of the proletarian park   in Coney Island where
my father saved up   to take me every
fourth of July back   when America was famous
for spacious skies, amber   waves of grain, liberty
and justice for all,   the funhouse mirrors could
expand and contract you,   lengthen and fatten you,

distort you but only   temporarily, because America was
a free country, we   could giggle at ourselves
and walk away, we   Jews were especially lucky
living in this free   country, a country without
pogroms, we could vote   we could defeat tyrants
and bigots we could   end segregation and poverty
and I can't quite   remember getting on the

train that brought us   to this funhouse where
the dim-lit corrugated latex   tunnel like the interior
of a large insect whips   us along waving tendrils
waving mirrors twisting our   images to images of
the king smiling at   us in our baskets
in the rushing Nile   loudly wailing and screaming
brown infant bodies bobbing   in the surrounding water

This chapter does not include the king's daughter

Chapter Four: The Message

"Sorry, the page you're looking for cannot be found," is the message Internet users receive when trying to access the Spanish version of the White House page. . . . Up until Jan. 20, the site also had a blog dedicated to issues considered of interest for the Hispanic community.

—FOX NEWS

"Sorry the page you are looking for cannot be found"

—MY LAPTOP SCREEN

Because there is nothing new under the sun
let's look for precedents: Emperor Shih Huang Ti
built the wall and burned the books
in the third century before Jesus so we have
an idea what to expect: say goodbye to the Spanish
language version of the White House web page
and the associated blogs thereof, goodbye to science
and jurisprudence, hello informers, hello more and more massive
accumulations of wealth, hello expanding gulag, hello to the songs
of resistance, the poems inscribed on toilet paper
and slivers of soap, memory sharpened
like a steak knife, all borders closed,
a time to wait. A time to refrain from waiting.

Chapter Five: In the Shadow of Liberty

Winter's been warm and rainy, here in the city,
although the day we marched, bright sunlight
filled millions of hearts already opened
to radical entries of hope and fear.

It was like this all over the planet—
we trust our hormones, we trust our women's
hearts like the open borders we march for,
sunlight, communal singing, clever signs,

Hope dominant, moms and dads, so many young—

then we go home and fear greets us in the kitchen,
we go to bed with fear, the cruel king
issues his ban, one more invisible
missile strikes Liberty, Mother of Exiles,

she who welcomed my grandparents
fleeing...by now, my son is preparing to spend
a weekend setting taps for our sugar maples
in Chester, Massachusetts, on our small piece

of the "natural world," and if I close

my eyes, I am there with him, it's sunny
and cold, maybe a dust of snow, we breathe
the sparkling air, we look around at pillars
of maple, pine and oak trunks, tangles of branches,

Leaves crunch under our feet,
fear leaves us, for a moment, and then
eyes open, I am back in the city, it's rainy
and I do not know how anything will end.

CODA: SUTRA

First   we dream of a new world
a new   heaven and a new   earth
being   born into time and space

we don't
know   from where
never   mind

The dream   is born   again and again
like a tree   in a rainforest   that burgeons
solemn green   its boughs

are home   to insect, owl
spring peeper   small mammal
It falls over and   makes no sound

because   nobody is there to hear it
in time   more than one tree   grows from its trunk
it had to fall   for this to happen

life surges from the corpse
of the old moldy fallen thing
leafing everywhere

time passes
and then   repeats

ACKNOWLEDGMENTS

The poems from *the volcano sequence* were deeply influenced by Jewish feminism in the United States and Canada, and in particular by Adrienne Rich, Judith Plaskow, Starhawk, Jill Hammer, and other women visionaries including H. D., Lucille Clifton, and Judy Grahn. I am indebted as well to the scholars Gershom Scholem, Rafael Patai, and Alana Pardes—and, always, to the language of the Bible, with which I have been wrestling in prose and poetry for several decades.

The poems from *At the Revelation Restaurant* originally appeared in my chapbook of that title published by Marick Press. My gratitude to Mariela Griffor, its publisher, and to Ilya Kaminsky who suggested our connection.

The poems from the "new" section of this volume originally appeared or will appear in *American Poetry Review, Prairie Schooner, Women's Review of Books, Plume, Solstice, Fifth Wednesday, Image, Smartish Pace, The Progressive, BigCityLit,, Barzakh, Great River, Poem-a-Day,* and *Tikkun.*

I am indebted to so many people who generously read stacks of poems, sometimes more than once. Your comments and advice have been boundlessly helpful. You all have had a finger in this pie, and I am grateful to you. In no particular order you include the women in the online wom-po group—Ann Fisher-Wirth, Penelope Schott, Louisa Howerow, Patricia Fargnoli, Athena Kildegaard, Wendy Carlisle Ann Hostetler—as well as my dear friends Martha Nell Smith, Toi Derricotte, Rebecca Payne Howell.Tess O'Dwyer, Wendy Barker, Mimi Schwartz, Peter Pitzele, and my wizard editor Ed Ochester. I am grateful to JPO for love, support, and companionship always, and for his sharp critic's eye on my prose and my photographs.